YOU DON'T KNOW SHEEP

An Unconventional Field Guide for Today's Faith Leader

David McCauley
with Melinda Folse

FIVE CROW PRESS™

You Don't Know Sheep: An Unconventional Field Guide for Today's Faith Leader

Copyright © 2024 by David McCauley

All rights reserved. No part of this book may be reproduced or utilized in any form or by any means, electronic or mechanical, including photocopying, recording, or by any information storage or retrieval systems, without permission in writing from the publisher. For information contact:

Five Crow Press
An imprint of The Folse Group, LLC
Fort Worth, Texas 76107
fivecrowpress.com

The publisher is not responsible for the content of websites not owned by the publisher. All website addresses were checked and verified to be correct at the time of publication. Because of the dynamic nature of the Web, some addresses may have changed since publication and may no longer be valid.

Library of Congress Control Number:
ISBN: 979-8-9897274-5-2

Design: Liphus M. Swindall

Printed in the United States of America

*I dedicate this book to the ones with Big Hearts,
who care about truly helping and loving on people, and
to all the modern-day shepherds trying to find a better path
to green pastures for the people they love and serve.*

"To love at all is to be vulnerable. Love anything, and your heart will certainly be wrung and possibly be broken. If you want to make sure of keeping it intact, you must give your heart to no one, not even to an animal. Wrap it carefully round with hobbies and little luxuries; avoid all entanglements; lock it up safe in the casket or coffin of your selfishness. But in that casket—safe, dark, motionless, airless—it will change. It will not be broken; it will become unbreakable, impenetrable, irredeemable."

— C.S. Lewis, *The Four Loves*

CONTENTS

PREFACE: You Think You Know Sheep? xiii

INTRODUCTION: Reimagine Shepherding xix
A shepherd is a person who protects, guides, and watches over an individual or a group. The relationship between shepherds and their flocks is one of love; they live together and walk through life together. That's basic leadership, right?

CHAPTER 1: Become a People Whisperer 1
When something goes wrong or people get stressed, how do you handle it? Looking to the immediate and visible feedback loops found in the natural world can help hone your skills of emotional self-control and leadership, enabling you to better serve your flock.

CHAPTER 2: Revisit Who Jesus Is 10
Ministry is filled with ego traps, and even well-intentioned leaders can fall into them. Leaders can take things on "for God" that are opposite of God's actual intent. How can you learn to let Jesus lead and the Holy Spirit do the hard work when the all-too-human desire is to save the day?

CHAPTER 3: Lead from Outside the Box 20
Leaders have to have vision and keep the big picture in mind at all times. However, when looking only at the big picture, you can miss what's going on at ground level and make judgments about people and situations without fully understanding the ins and outs—what's *really* happening—and this can have unintended results.

CHAPTER 4: Distill the Paradox 29
The acute stress of too many choices can short-circuit our brains from goal-directed to habit-based decision-making. The secret is to consider the outcomes, learning to compare the value of the rewards on the other side of each choice—and stay focused when too many options overwhelm.

CHAPTER 5: Unpack How People Respond. 35
Today's church leaders have to learn to recognize what lies beneath a bluster of emotion in order to keep relationships thriving. Many people carry some level of emotional trauma. Understanding how coping mechanisms can be the drivers of primal reactions can help leaders respond to pushback against their vision and equip people to thrive.

CHAPTER 6: Reevaluate "Scary People" 51
People with nothing to lose are sometimes considered "scary," but they can also be the ones who change the world. If you could do anything, with nothing to lose, what would you do?

CHAPTER 7: Crystalize Intent 64
Having a vision will only take you so far. Intent is the engine that powers your vision. Clarifying your intent (even somewhat loosely) is the foundation for generating ideas and evolving a plan for you and your church. Intent transforms your vision into reality.

CHAPTER 8: Empower a Hierarchy Flow 73
As a leader, your primary job is keeping your ministry, your people, and your projects aligned with what God wants. When passion and resources don't align, it's time to use a prescribed process of employing creative limitations and learning to let go in positive ways.

CHAPTER 9: Guide the Experience 92
As a shepherd, your job is not only to protect and care for the flock, you are the guide responsible for making the knowledge, assurance, and lifestyle God offers accessible. The choices you make about your worship space guide the experience of the people you serve.

CHAPTER 10: Tap into the Power of Music **110**
It's no secret that integrating music into faith services provides a connector and an enhancement for learning. Strong leadership, intentional focus, and thoughtful choices for presenting music in worship can bridge generational, cultural, and language gaps.

CHAPTER 11: Reclaim the Practice of Rest **119**
Ministry is exhausting work and there's never enough time to get everything done. (Who has time to rest?) But rest is important. By remembering and honoring rest as one of the Ten Commandments, you can restore a life-giving rhythm to your life and ministry—for the long run.

CHAPTER 12: Remember Your Why **131**
God has purposely put you in the place you're in, with people in whom God also dwells. There's something extraordinary God wants to do through each of them, and it's your job to prepare them to be transformative. The secret to this work is elegant in its simplicity.

AFTERWORD: Now that You Know Sheep **141**

About the Author **151**

Acknowledgments **153**

PREFACE
You Think You Know Sheep?

Who Am I and Why Did I Write This Book?

I have thirty-something years of experience working in professional theater and live production, and I've used creative ingenuity to help find out-of-the-box solutions in acoustics, audio imaging, projection, and staging for hundreds of churches, ministries, and performance venues of all sizes across the nation. This experience, paired with my innate curiosity (and stoked by collegiate studies in both psychology and theology), has given me a unique perspective on the people, venues, and leadership dynamics I've encountered day in and day out for more than three decades.

Over the years, what I had thought were isolated incidents and personal quirks of the leaders around me began to emerge as patterns. They reminded me of the fractal patterns found in nature—those patterns that repeat over and over again, where the shapes of the smaller parts of the pattern resemble the shapes of the larger parts of the whole. (Think of the infinite Fibonacci sequence. It begins with 1 and 1, and each succeeding number is the sum of the two numbers immediately preceding. In nature, this is represented in the predictable growth-spiral sequence found in things like tree branches, pine cones, seashells, and, in my opinion, spiritual growth.) I began to wonder why the same dynamics were playing out again and again for church leaders in all denominations and with congregations of all sizes. Could there be biblical reasons for these dynamics?

In the hurry-up-and-wait nature of my business, I tend to have a lot of time on my hands to think about these things. This book is the culmination and distillation of all that thinking, having spent years both observing human nature and thinking about the nature of God in these situations. It provides a plan for how church leaders can marshal these dynamics to successfully lead the congregations and faith organizations of today.

You opened this book, possibly flipped through it, and maybe you laughed a bit at the title and graphics. Maybe you saw a few things that intrigued you. So, you bought it, and here we are. Whether you are leading a group of thousands or a few individuals; if you're the head of a company, a church, a worship team, or a youth group; or if your leadership role is helping to guide a brother, sister, friend, or even someone you just met, the observations and insights in this book will empower you to both lead and be led. Whoever and wherever you are in your life, you will be able to apply these tools to the situations you face in which you feel the nudge to step up.

The title of this book, *You Don't Know Sheep*, started out as just a funny little inside joke I made (to myself, of course) when I noticed church leadership missing opportunities with their congregations. The joke originated long before that, though, when the seed of a book idea was planted early in my career. I spent some of my formative years working in live theater, including at a major theater in Lancaster, Pennsylvania, called Sight & Sound Theatres, which had a lot of live animals in their productions. (We're talking horses, goats, cats, dogs, lamas, camels—yes, they spit *and* can kick straight sideways!—oxen, cows, birds, and also sheep. *Lots* of sheep.) I've always known that in the Bible, God refers to us as sheep. And that, at the time the biblical texts were written, dealing with sheep was a common thing; everyone had access to or at least some experience with sheep. But in today's world, a lot of biblical metaphors are not so obvious. In fact, who among us has spent much real time with sheep? Not me! I'm a city boy, and even though I love animals and know something about horses and dogs, sheep are . . . sort of a mystery. Yet, as a student of theology, I recognize the concept of sheep as a principal understanding that underpins this recurring biblical metaphor.

So I'm at the Sight & Sound Theatres working, we have some down time, and I'm sitting on the stage reading. I had been studying some material relevant to leadership and God and how leaders communicated in biblical times versus now, and I start watching the sheep.

They're falling into the lighting pit, time after time (this was many years ago—I'm sure this would never be allowed to happen now). They'd fall, then cry out for help, and the handlers would come get them out. One sheep was tied up, but he got himself all tangled and had to be freed. Another was just meddling around and got caught up in stuff he shouldn't have. As I watched this unfold, the parallel hit me. I laughed out loud. In the Bible, we are referred to as the sheep and Jesus as the Good Shepherd.

That's when I started really watching the behavior and antics of these sheep. I noticed they were actually kind of cute. They were harmless, vulnerable, and very malleable animals. (God's sense of humor really shines in the sheep parallel.) My next observations were less kind. The sheep were always getting themselves in trouble, distracted, not paying attention. I watched them, time after time, falling into the lighting pit, getting stuck in the cords and cables that littered the set, or wandering away for seemingly no reason. The livestock handlers (performing as "shepherd") had a full-time job on their hands just keeping the sheep from hurting themselves. They did this by rescuing them over and over again, guiding them out of harm's way, and putting up barriers to keep them from things that would hurt them.

The other thing I noticed was the trail of (literal) crap sheep leave wherever they go. This is not a big mess, like horse or cow manure, but it's just constant. A path of thousands of little pellets so you can always tell where they have been. Just follow the trail of crap. At this point I was laughing so hard it was starting to draw attention from others on the set around me. As I waved them off (don't mind me, I'm just having a hilarious epiphany over here!), I said to myself, "Wow, we *are* just like sheep. We are always in some sort of trouble, whether it's self-inflicted or from outside forces, and, left to our own devices, the choices we make are usually going to make matters worse or be just plain dangerous. Not to mention everywhere we go as a society we leave a wake of crap for someone else to clean up.

Then it hit me: How crucially important leadership is for any flock, and how church leaders, like the handlers on that stage, are called to play this role of shepherd. Every leader of every congregation or faith organization is charged with keeping watch over those in their care, training them to listen for God's voice as they seek comfort, safety, and security. It was suddenly like I was sitting at the feet of Jesus, soaking up this concept and context—but it would be decades before I knew how I would gather it into this book.

Why Read This Book?

Understanding the dynamics of faith-based leadership is the key to success, whether you're leading a church, mentoring a team, teaching children, or befriending individuals who have lost their way. Before you can ever grasp a concept, you must look at the *why*, and this book will offer you tools for unpacking the key leadership concepts that will give you better insight into your own *why* of leadership. More importantly, it will give you better insight into how to get to the *why* of those you're called to lead.

This is a book for leaders and for anyone who aspires to lead. What I want you to know right here from the start is that if you guide or care for anyone for any reason, you are leading them. Leading and mentoring boils down to just that—guiding and caring. It's looking out for the well-being, best interests, and ultimate good of an individual or group. It's a lot like herding sheep.

Am I calling people sheep? Am I saying people are dumb or anything like that? No! The focus of this book is the dynamic of caring, thoughtful, conscientious leadership from the biblical perspective of the shepherd. The parallels are many, and I've grouped my stories, observations, and reflections, as well as a few actionable prompts and takeaways, into twelve chapters.

This book is my gift to you, a labor of love and a humbling confessional. It's a compilation of experiences God has led me through over the past few decades. As a dedicated observer of God's creation, I believe I've stumbled upon some important insights into the way God has created us, and how God wants us to respond to the opportunities we face. (And they're *all* opportunities, really—some of them just feel better than others.) I'm not some special, high-level know-it-all. I'm just someone in the trenches who said "Yes" to God's call, and who wants to share my observations of what God has shown me through the experiences that have shaped my life up to this point.

Remember, although most people don't think of themselves as leaders, if you guide anyone for any reason, you are leading them. I think the observations in this book will not only help you to lead, but will also help you to be led. I am going to focus on helping people learn to apply the leadership tools in this book to wherever and for whomever they are leading.

Do You Know What I Mean?

If you've ever been around me, you know I have a verbal tic of asking that question incessantly as I'm trying to explain something. I think it began as my way of making sure people understood what I was saying and that they were still with me as we waded through the ins and outs of sound and lighting design. (Tech details are not always as riveting to others as they are to me, so I always wanted to be sure I wasn't losing attention span in these conversations.) While this question has become a point of familiarity for family, friends, and clients, it also serves a purpose in this book.

I get it. You're busy. You probably don't have a lot of free time to read, think, or ponder the underpinnings of your leadership—just like most people never have to (or really want to) think about how light and sound in a given spaces influences the absorption of a message. You just want to flip a few switches, do what you do, and know that the people you lead have heard, absorbed, and will benefit from it. I think that's also the way it is with leadership, especially leadership in a church or faith-based organization. We show up, we deal with the challenges and opportunities of every day, and we do our best—isn't that enough?

Well, yes and no. God's going to love us no matter what we do. But the people we lead are depending on us to show them the way. To understand and take care of their needs—and to lead them in such a way that they feel safe, cared for, and on the right path. That's where thinking about, delving into, understanding, and applying the principles I bring to you in this book can make a difference in how you lead, where you lead from, and the difference you can make in the lives you serve. Isn't that what it's all about?

So, at the end of each chapter you'll find a little section of questions with the title, "Do You Know What I Mean?" to help boil down the biggest ideas of each chapter, invite you to relate them to your own life and situation, and serve as a prompt for how you might apply them to your own life and leadership. I invite you to at least read them and, if you feel inspired, grab a notebook (nothing fancy—this is a brain dump. You never know what's hiding in there until you start writing!). Do a little journaling on each question. You might be surprised at the new ideas and innate wisdom that pop out.

INTRODUCTION

Reimagine Shepherding

*Once we're aware of the richness of this metaphor,
we can begin to more fully understand what
God wants us to know about leadership in churches.*

■

Let's start with the spiritual overseer: the pastor. The word *pastor* is from the Latin word for "shepherd." This person protects, guides, and watches over an individual or a group. That's basic leadership, right?

In the tenth chapter of the Gospel of John we find the shepherd and sheep metaphor in a discussion about how and why sheep follow their shepherd's voice. Sheep follow the voice because they know it when they hear it. Even more important, the shepherd knows the sheep—how to care for them, what they need, how they behave, what motivates them, what frightens them, and how to manage them effectively when unanticipated, unpredictable, and unsettling things inevitably happen to them over the course of their lives.

I've worked with hundreds of church leaders over the years in many different capacities (mostly in designing lighting, sound, and audiovisual systems) to help them deliver their messages in the most impactful way for the physical space they're in. I've worked with churches across the United States and around the globe, and with church leaders of all denominations who have faith communities of all sizes. And I've found very few who really know their congregation in a deep, intimate way. How they operate. What makes them tick. What brings them excitement, joy, sadness, and fear. What motivates them from the highest levels of their consciousness. When frustrated, many of these leaders fall back on old dogma to try and get the job done as quickly and as easily as possible. Sometimes they completely miss opportunities to ask questions crucial to discovering what God intends for their leadership.

The Role of Shepherd

In Matthew 10 we're told to "go rather to the lost sheep." Go rather to the lost sheep? Rather than what? I've always wondered what the other option was. This biblical metaphor of us as sheep kept getting funnier and more apropos the more I learned about these animals. Here are a few tidbits to help cement the humor in this metaphor for you too (I bet you recognize some, if not all, of these traits in your own congregation!):

- Sheep are very gregarious, caring, and social.
- Sheep like to congregate and stay close to the other members of their flock.
- Sheep are prey animals. (1 Peter warns us that there's always something out to devour them.)
- Sheep have a natural tendency to develop a hierarchy.
- Sheep will follow their trusted leader to new pastures or wherever they are led, good or bad. (Psalm 23 says this even includes "the valley of the shadow of death." That's some heavy stuff!)
- Sheep need to keep moving to different pastures; if they stop too long, they kill their environment, run out of food, and starve.
- If sheep stay in the same pasture too long, parasites can wreak havoc; if they keep moving, they interrupt the parasite gestation cycles.
- Sheep panic easily when dealing with stressful situations, and the first thing they do is run towards the safety of the flock and hope that the leader shows them the way out of danger.
- It is better to lead sheep from the front, having them follow, so they will stay focused on the shepherd and not on the scary things all around them. (1 Corinthians echoes this advice for how we are to follow Jesus.)

- When sheep run out of food, they start to wander in search of more food.
- When sheep get too comfortable, they start spreading out too far, apart from the flock. (Guess what happens when trouble comes? Or when a different flock goes by? Oh boy! The circus!)

The relationship between shepherds and their flocks is one of love; they live together and walk through life together. Sheep are able to recognize their shepherd's voice from a distance, they know their shepherd's face if they see it, and they know their shepherd's scent if they smell it. Moreover, the shepherd knows the sheep; their names, the noises they make, how they look, and how they act. Shepherds know more about their sheep than the sheep know about themselves.

Also in the Bible are goats. I want to be clear that this tidbit has nothing to do with Jesus separating the sheep from the goats in the Gospel of Matthew—even though inserting the observation here may appear to hint at that. This is just a note about the nature of some of the animals mentioned in the Bible and the possible metaphors that can be drawn from them, taking into account the context of the historical time the Bible was written.

There is an interesting distinction between goats and sheep. As has already been mentioned, sheep are cute, quiet, gentle, caring, and trusting. They are easily led and don't start trouble. Aside from their (many) innocent blunders, sheep are pretty easy to watch over. Goats, on the other hand, are a handful. Goats always push the limits—and they are always in some sort of trouble or deliberate mischief. Goats do not stay in flocks like sheep. Instead, they spread out and go their own way. Keeping goats safe means spending lots of time chasing them, actively herding them out of the trouble of their own making. If you've ever found yourself in a situation where leadership is unusually challenging, when a group is particularly hard to corral, the dynamics of dealing with a herd of goats could come in handy.

I love this quote by a goat owner: "Goats just like to go wherever they think you don't want them to go." Goats are very inquisitive and they will eat or try to eat just about anything. They will explore new things and spaces, and climb seemingly everything within reach. Goats are escape artists, and they will find and exploit any weakness in a fence or other boundary until they're free. Goats think that they are in control. They explore on their own, and when a predator comes near, they turn to face the predator alone rather than running to the safety of the herd. It's not that goats are bad, they just don't like being led. If you're watching over a goat, it's going to be harder to connect.

Because goats and sheep are related (they share the same subfamily *Caprinae*) and have some of the same physical features, people tend to lump them into the same categories and assume they have the same behavior characteristics. But the same rules do not apply to both species. Camels and horses (also in the Bible) are another pairing of animals some assume behave the same way. Although both animals are ridden and used for transport, they have distinct behavioral differences. And until you know them, you don't. The shepherds in biblical times knew all of this. They understood what Jesus meant when he drew these animal parallels and the context of the references. These animal relationships and behaviors were familiar to them. They are God's observations of our own human tendencies.

Sheep and goats, while fundamentally different, are equally intelligent and messy. While sheep will follow their shepherd, know their shepherd's voice, focus on community, and respect boundaries, they are easily distracted and can quickly (and inadvertently) find themselves in trouble. Goats are going to do their own thing, follow their own ideas about what is best and—according to longtime goat owners—without close supervision and watchful intervention, there's a good chance they may even die from their own bad choices. Both sheep and goats require solid leadership.

A quick word about camels. I don't know if you've ever been around camels, but I spent a lot of time personally observing them while working at Sight & Sound Theatres in Pennsylvania. They are big and strong and ornery! They can do things that you may not expect, like kick you from the side (not just from behind like a horse). Most of the time, the first thing people say about camels is that they spit, and that is true. They do. And it is not fun to be spit on by a camel. But what most people don't know about camels is they have a much sneakier attack. They have a tuft of hair at the end of their tail that they love to hit people with as they walk by (ask me how I know this), and this is bad enough, but the real surprise is that they like to pee on that part right before they hit you with it! Bottom line? Camels always get the last laugh.

Shepherds Got the Joke—Now We Can, Too!

When the full meaning of the tongue-in-cheek sheep metaphor—we as the sheep, Jesus as the Good Shepherd—really hit me, I appreciated God's sense of humor as never before. I understood what God was saying. Those early shepherds got the joke, too, because they *did* know sheep. Sheep were as much a part of their culture as driving a car is a part of ours. In today's world, however, I think most people blow right past this key metaphorical parallel for leaders and those being led. We think we're in control. Meanwhile, God looks at us as if to say: "Sure, they're kind of cute, and pretty smart, but they just don't know how to keep themselves out of trouble. They need someone to look out for them. Like constantly."

Realizing this made me laugh. Even after that moment, when I first got the joke, it still took me twenty-five years to unpack it for today's leader. We hear, say, and talk about leadership all the time in church and in other faith-based organizations, but we can't fully understand the true leadership dynamic without having the context. We don't know sheep. And that's okay. Unless you live on a farm, you have no reason to! But now that we're aware of the richness of this metaphor, we can begin to more fully understand what God wants us to know about leadership.

People want and need good leadership. We were designed from the beginning to be led—by God. However, in the beginning, God's people wanted something different. In Old Testament times, they decided they wanted to be led by a king. So all the elders went to the prophet Samuel and said he was too old to lead them. They asked him to appoint a king as their leader. When Samuel, who was displeased by this, prayed to God about it, God told Samuel to listen to them, but also to warn them about what a king would claim as his rights. Even after Samuel follows God's directions and warns the people what having a king would mean, explaining to them what the king would demand from them and providing a long list of all the things a king will require of them, they double down and demand a king to rule over them.

When the people asked to be led, specifically by a king, God's response was more or less, "Well . . .okay . . ." But the people were certain they wanted a king. They *wanted* to be led. The complexity of this interaction and dynamic of leadership is what got me going on this book.

Do You Know What I Mean?

- Looking at the narrative sweep of the Bible, do you see the pattern of people in trouble, God saving them, people in trouble, God saving them . . . all the way through the final act?

- When have you seen that pattern play out in your own life, in your congregation, in the lives of people you serve?

- The voice we listen for and follow as leaders, God's voice, is loving and familiar to us and we know that if we follow it, we will remain on our best path. How can you teach others to listen for that voice? How can you echo that voice for people who have lost their way?

CHAPTER 1
Become a People Whisperer

"This is as loud as I will get."
—Tony Dungy
(Address to the Indianapolis Colts, January 2002)

∎

One of the biggest lessons I've learned about healthy leadership is to take emotion out of things. This can be very hard to do when having faith-related conversations, because passion and emotion are always just under the surface of every interaction.

I learned this lesson from an old cowboy named Terry. Love him or hate him, Terry was a very smart guy in his own way. Being smart about handling horses equipped Terry to be smart about people, too. (This is the case for a lot of horse trainers, but that's another story for another day.) Was Terry a horse whisperer? No, I would call Terry the opposite of a horse whisperer—more like a horse yeller! But the reason for Terry's somewhat obnoxious volume was a little different than what you might think. Terry knew that although loud sounds can and do spook horses, horses read people from the inside; they don't react as much to sound as they do to our underlying emotional energy.

Terry, who worked part-time as a dude-ranch guide, would take a group of novice riders, put them on horses, and take them out onto the trails on all sorts of terrain. The horses Terry used were not old, broken-down, and lifeless. These horses were full of life—and that was both good and bad. Many of the people who came to ride with Terry thought they were experts. How hard can it be, right? If you've ridden one or two trail horses in your life, participated in a riding module at summer camp, or habitually hopped aboard amusement park carousels, you know how to ride? Not so much. And time after time on these rides I heard people upset with the horse they were riding:

> "This horse won't listen."
> "This horse won't slow down!"
> "This horse won't go."
> "This horse can't keep up with the others!"

I always smiled to myself when I heard these complaints. As anyone who knows anything about horses will tell you, it's rarely, if ever, the horse's fault. Horse problems are almost always people problems in disguise.

On one trip, things got weird with this couple. Both of them were having big-time trouble with their horses. Normally when this happened, we would switch out their horses and it'd be fine. Whenever the person riding was stressed out, that stress was reflected in the horse's behavior. And, because some horses are just more sensitive than others, changing horses usually solved this problem. But not that day. Terry decided instead to use this opportunity to make a point. He picked a fight with these people. Not a real fight, of course. He just started mouthing off, saying obnoxious, sexist things like men are better than women at riding and nonsense stuff like that. I knew he didn't really believe any of the stuff he was spouting off, but it got the reaction he was going for.

When both the man and the woman in this couple reacted to his remarks, all the focus—of people and horses alike—went to Terry. All of a sudden, he became the leader. The horses stopped responding to the energy of the people riding them and began to follow what their rider was paying attention to. As each person's focus and energy shifted to Terry, and they were suddenly too busy arguing with this crazy person to remember they were even *on* a horse, their horses settled down. It was a magical thing to watch.

After a bit, Terry would circle back to the person and say something encouraging like, "You're doing good, look at that horse now, listening and going great!" If their attention and energy started getting fractious again, he'd say something else to keep their attention focused.

Now, to be clear, I'm not recommending this as a leadership technique—amazing as it was to witness that day. The takeaway from this story is that when something went wrong and people got stressed, Terry didn't say a word about that. He just came alongside and took charge, pulling the focus away from the issue at hand.

You can see these kinds of leadership lessons easily with horses because they are flight animals and therefore extremely sensitive to emotional triggers. And working with horses can really hone your skills pertaining to emotional control and leadership because the feedback is both immediate and very visible. They're 1,000-pound animals. Nothing they do is small. As famous horseman Ray Hunt was well-known for saying about learning from horses: "Everything means something, and nothing means nothing."

Fundamental Designs in Group Dynamics

At our most basic level, we are all designed to operate in certain ways. Physical stimuli directs either action or reaction. There are countless studies to document this and also many examples found throughout history. Many examples can also be found in biblical history. I recently heard someone say that in modern times we are much more likely to teach the Bible as a collection of stories rather than as history—meaning that biblical history has become more about observation and lessons than historical fact. The reality is, it's both. And so much more. Biblical history shows us the sweeping totality of man's relationship with God—and the true nature of God as revealed in Jesus. If we look closely at the historical context of the stories in the Bible, we'll be continually amazed at the deeper truths revealed that are as relevant today as they were in that time.

Getting to the topic of people whispering—how to get people to listen to you—I return to the natural world to talk about the concept of pressure. (At some point we'll get back to the sheep, but we're going to stay with the horses for just a little longer.) Monty Roberts, one of the first to be called a "horse whisperer" in our popular culture, studied horses both as a domestic horse trainer and as an observer of horses in the wild. He experimented with different types of pressure techniques to help horses learn to trust him.

Roberts grew up with horses. His father was a horse trainer who was pretty rough and used strong training methods to *force* a horse to comply with his wishes. This harsher type of fear-based training, long part of old-time cowboy culture, seemed to work, and some in the horse world still use it today, but the younger Roberts realized that that fear—particularly fear of pain—was not the only way to train a horse. Following his intuitive insight, Roberts began watching horses and observing how they worked as a group. He learned that they did things as a herd, and that the horses wanted to be in the herd for both safety and social reasons. He also observed that to be a part of a herd they had to comply with the rules of that herd. The horses learned the lessons of the herd through pressure, tension, and leadership.

Roberts continued to study the social hierarchy of the herd, and from these observations he drew insights about how people tend to operate in groups. Not only is Roberts credited with sparking an entire movement in horse training called "natural horsemanship," but he later translated these leadership experiences with horses into strategies for working with troubled (human) youth. Roberts cracked the code of how social structures are created and how healthy parameters create stronger bonds built on trust.

What Roberts noticed and put into play with horses and people taps into how everyone operates to a certain extent. How we are all connected to the natural world and to each other. Jesus knew these parallels in creation, and that's why he used nature in his examples. There are certain dynamics that resonate throughout creation, and in understanding how these dynamics work, we can build better relationships, clearer social structures, and stronger groups.

If you can tolerate one more animal metaphor regarding leadership and group dynamics, sheepdogs also know how to use pressure effectively to move a herd. While a shepherd leads sheep from the front, giving them a singular focus and voice to follow, dogs guide and direct sheep differently. Unlike the shepherd, they use their eyes, position, and body language to put pressure on certain sheep in order to move the whole herd. Isn't that how people influence other people? God is the shepherd, and we focus on and follow that voice of God. Meanwhile, people—through cultural norms, social media influencers, and even friends and family to some extent—are circling around, nipping at our heels, pressuring us in one direction or another. That's the world, using the fear of pain to control our behavior. God is still out in front, inviting us to listen for His voice—to follow and focus on Him.

Pleasure Vs. Need

When we begin to think of following God as a pleasure (I'm inclined to follow, as it brings me joy), rather than a need (terrible things will happen if I don't), everything in life becomes rooted in good. As it says in Romans 8, when we focus on our love for God and following our unique call, all things will work together for good—even if that's hard to see in real time!

Following God takes the pressure off because it's rooted in goodness and pleasure, even in times that don't look or feel so good. It's there. Wait for it. When we realize we're not following God out of fear or to avoid pain, the world opens up and becomes a different place—a place of love and acceptance—of ourselves and others.

Some people think of God's voice as a judgmental voice. One of high expectations, one that criticizes our actions, one that beats us up for our choices. That's not God. It's easy to get trapped in that voice because we are hardwired to hear the negative over the positive. According to the National Science Foundation, 80 percent of our thoughts are negative and 95 percent of our thoughts are repetitive. Don't ask me why—it just is.

According to the National Institutes of Health, neuroscientists have studied for years this phenomenon they call *negativity bias*— or "the propensity to attend to, learn from, and use negative information far more than positive information." They describe this bias as "asymmetry in how adults use positive versus negative information to make sense of their world." Negativity bias is repeatedly revealed in judgment and decision-making. People consistently weigh the negative aspects of something more heavily than they do the positive. This bias is also present in their formation of impressions. When forming an overall impression of a person they don't know, after being given equal amounts of positive and negative information, people process and use the negative information more than they do the positive (Amrisha Vaish, Tobias Grossmann, and Amanda Woodward, "Not all emotions are created equal: The negativity bias in social-emotional development," National Institutes of Health. Article available at the National Library of Medicine, https://www.ncbi.nlm.nih.gov/pmc/articles/PMC3652533/).

Even when we're following God, the negative voices and thoughts surrounding us are constantly applying pressure, vying for our attention and focus.

What Can We Do About It?

Listen for the voice of love, encouragement, and strength. That's the voice we should be listening for and following. If it's not a caring voice, a loving voice, it's not God. That's not *your* shepherd talking. Just as we are assured in Isaiah 41, God promises to help us—not abandon us—when we're in need.

The thing is, God doesn't love us more when we get better, do better, climb higher, or accomplish more. God loves us completely now *and* when we do those things—there's no difference. God will love and encourage us *through* our accomplishments and endeavors, and regardless of the outcome, God's love never changes. Now, that's not to say we shouldn't try harder, do better, and achieve the most we can with what we've been given to work with.

Accomplishing things, reaching goals, and making changes for the better will open up new and better opportunities for us. When we learn how to use what we have been given and work hard to make the most of our opportunities, we earn access to even more of the good things God has for us. Nevertheless, God loves us fully and the same, no matter what we do or don't do.

People sometimes say, "I don't want to believe in God. I have so many more choices if I am not a Christian." *Do*, you? As a follower of Jesus, I can choose everything anyone else in the world can choose. And I can also choose to go to a loving God to rest and be comforted—and to seek wisdom. I can choose rest (more on that later), knowing God has things under control. I can ruin my life just like anyone else. As a follower of Jesus, I still have *all* the choices non-followers have, but then I also have others. I can choose to follow God for the comfort, pleasure, and safety it brings me, not out of the need to avoid punishment or to avoid the bad things that will inevitably come my way. My comfort and strength in good and bad, success and failure, sink and swim, all come from my choice to listen for and follow the voice of love.

Just a Few More Animals Before We Move On

If you're thinking, "Now, wait a minute. What does any of this have to do with leading churches? My congregation is not made up of horses or dogs or even actual sheep!" I'm here to tell you that God created everything to work in systems, in harmony. As humans, at the top of the intelligence chain, we're part of the same harmony God created for the other living beings in the natural world. Same creator, same creation.

Dogs and cats are predators and horses, sheep, and goats are prey. Yet, despite these differences, they share a lot of similar social behavior within their group dynamics. I like looking at these group dynamics because I see some similarities and parallels with groups of people I've observed. (Has anyone else ever looked around a conference table during a too-long meeting and tried to imagine what kind of animal each person would be if they were animals?) Depending on our personal characteristics and style, some people may favor predator traits (aggression, focus, steps up to confrontation), and others may have and be drawn to more prey-like tendencies (intuition, sensitivity, conflict avoidance). People can also be a mixture of both, and sometimes that is where experience and training have kicked in, and that's a different story altogether.

The point is, a big part of leadership is understanding these individual and group dynamics and flowing with them. It can be hard to see an immediate response in people who have a fixed mindset; it can take a really long time to make a change. However, with others you can see the difference almost immediately (with the right leadership).

I love the show *Dog Whisper with Cesar Millan,* which aired from 2004 to 2012. I think what most people don't get about this show—and possibly the most interesting thing to watch—is that in each episode the dog doesn't change nearly as dramatically as the dog owner does. More than just training dogs, Millan is teaching the people how to be leaders. On this show, and in most unhealthy organizations, it's the "leaders"—the people in charge—who are actually causing all the problems. When you look at this show through this lens and think about the dogs as a microcosm of your own little team (or pack or family), you can see some very interesting things.

Again, I'm very aware that dogs are not people. I *know* it is a lot more complicated with people, and you do have to do some things differently. Nevertheless, the basic dynamics are the same. The necessity for confidence in leadership is the same, and the asking for and rewarding good behavior—not bad—is key. Excitement, whether good or bad, is always a rewarding reaction.

Opposing Ways to Lead

I have come across accounts of many different styles of leadership. One style is what a lot of us do. The leaders have good intentions, but then fall back into old habits of least resistance—leading people through fear and intimidation—even when it doesn't make us feel good and isn't a healthy dynamic. Yes, some of these old-style tactics may work in the short term, but are they the best way?

In his 2021 Masterclass, film director James Cameron reflected on his own bad behavior early in his career, when he was still new at directing and things were not getting done in a timely fashion. He learned that when he got really mad and blew up at some people, *wow,* things got done! However, after some time passed, productivity would start lagging again. He thought nothing would get done without his flying off the handle. Although this proved correct, when he realized it was his bad behavior that was being rewarded, he decided to work to change his behavior.

On the other end of the leadership-style spectrum is former NFL player and coach Tony Dungy, someone I consider to be a primo people whisperer. Dungy served as head coach of the Tampa Bay Buccaneers for six seasons and as head coach of the Indianapolis Colts for seven. As a professional football coach, his teams were perennial post-season contenders. (Under his leadership, the Bucs only missed the playoffs twice!) Dungy said that in a place where the norm was to yell and scream at people, he did the opposite. In 2002, addressing the Colts as their new head coach, Dungy spoke in a plain conversational voice: "This is as loud as I will get," he said.

Just like with the old-time horse trainers mentioned earlier, Dungy emphasized that while extreme measures may get the job done, abuse is not healthy on either side of the equation. Without question, many championships have been won—and organizations built—with these verbally abusive methods, but at what cost to the mental, physical, and spiritual well-being of those involved?

Understanding leadership dynamics and how people are wired is crucial to reconditioning on both sides: a new way to lead and a new way of being led. These dynamics and changes are apparent in the animal world because the results happen so fast. Blowing up in anger may stop a behavior, but will not help individuals grow, understand, and feel safe. Angry, emotional responses can backfire in other ways, too. Key to leadership success is learning the tools of calm redirection. This will allow you to keep control of your own emotions, even when others are losing their ever-loving minds. These dynamics are at work when training animals, when raising kids, and when leading entire organizations. They are simple to identify, but hard to master.

Do You Know What I Mean?

- When have you witnessed the dynamics of contrasting leadership styles in your personal life, business, and ministry?

- Have you ever caught yourself leading in a way you're not proud of, maybe resorting to old-school intimidation and scare tactics to get the behavior change you want?

- What could you do differently to lead people using pressure and reinforcement instead?

CHAPTER 2
Revisit Who Jesus Is

When we get all amped up thinking we've got to protect Jesus, we're trying to become the hero, the savior, rather than allowing Jesus and the Holy Spirit to work through us.

■

There's really nothing like having your face planted against a wall with a pistol pointed at the base of your skull to help you rethink your choices.

As a relatively new Christian, I was still running with a rough crowd, continuing the rock-and-roll lifestyle. God had gotten hold of me, and now I was on a mission to find the lost and get them into the arms of Christ. On this particular day, I had called a friend (we'll call him John, to protect his privacy), who I believed God was chasing. I think I had prayed for him, but he was still living in the same mess, and still running from God. I had told John about the 1981 "Hound of Heaven" song by Daniel Amos and how I thought the lyric "you can run, you can't hide from the hound of heaven" was true, that the hound of heaven nipping at his heels would continue until he made a different choice for his life. I reminded John that there is an easy way and a hard way to answer God's call.

Now I want to take a moment to introduce you to a Yiddish term. I'm not Jewish, but I appreciate how Yiddish so often provides us with the best descriptors for things we can't otherwise name. The term is *schmegge*, meaning "nonsense" or "baloney." I borrow this term to describe that instant when you think you have everything under control and God pulls the chair of certainty you were sitting on right out from under you. You've been there. We all have.

The Old Testament story of Jonah offers a perfect example of *schmegge*. Jonah, who thinks he is escaping God's instruction to go to Nineveh, heads in the opposite direction in a boat. He is then washed overboard in a storm and swallowed by a whale who promptly swims to the sandy beaches of Nineveh and pukes him right onto Nineveh's shore, the very place Jonah was trying to avoid. *Schmegge.*

Going back to my predicament (remember, my face is against a wall with a gun to my head), I had called John to invite him to a live music event. John had recently decided to follow Christ, maybe in part because of our conversations, but he still wasn't ready to give up his lifestyle. At the time I was clueless about this. (Sometimes these insights come along much later. Sometimes they never do.)

"Hey," I said. "Do you want to go to a concert at church today?"

"Sure!" he said. "Can you come pick me up?"

"Of course!" I said, and then we agreed on a time.

I went to John's apartment to pick him up, and, as usual, he wasn't quite ready. So, I was sitting there on his sofa while he was in the shower, and there was a knock at the door. I answered it, and BAM! I was up against the wall before I knew what hit me.

Oh boy, I thought, *here we go.* I was not unfamiliar with this type of roughness, but fortunately it had never found me personally. Until now—after I had changed my ways and became a Christian. The irony did not escape me. *Schmegge.*

Thankfully, I soon realized it was a police officer on the other end of the gun. Not that I liked being cuffed and having guns pointed at me by anyone, but it was a relief for it to have been the police, not a retaliating drug dealer or overheated debt collector. When John walked out of the bathroom, he, too, got the thrill of looking down the barrels of a few guns.

"Well, John," I said as we were sitting there under the supervision of armed police officers while his apartment was being searched, "it looks like the hounds have caught up to you." *Schmegge*, part deux.

Long story short, this was a changing point in John's life. (Mine, too, to some extent, as I experienced an unforgettable truth of how God works in us and in others.) I tried my best to be a friend and love John through the jail time that ensued and some other things that happened. To this day he is a dedicated and productive follower of Christ.

I say all this not to brag, but to make sure that one thing is clear: It is not our job to change people's minds, to convince them that we are right and they are wrong. It is well-documented that the less people know something they're saying is true, the louder and harder they will argue.

This Hound Is *Relentless*—in a Good Way!

Predestination is the doctrine that God already has knowledge of all events, knows our fates, and guides those who are destined for salvation. I don't agree with this belief in full, but one thing about predestination I do believe is that we are all chased by "the hound of heaven" mentioned in the Daniel Amos song based on the poem written in 1890 by Francis Thompson. (Look it up: http://www.houndofheaven.com/poem.) That poem really speaks to how the least and the lost ache for redemption in the midst of the chaos of their own making. The hound in this instance is the Lord, who continues to seek us out, even though we may continue to run in the opposite direction.

Like Jonah, who ended up at Nineveh despite his efforts to be elsewhere, we might be asked to do something we're not in favor of—and we run the other way. Depending on the task, God will send the "hound of heaven" (more in the form of nagging thoughts). It will nip at your heels until you are tired enough to say, "Okay, God, I don't like it, but I'll do it."

This might mean forgiving someone you're still angry with, or it might mean something bigger, like accepting Jesus as your Savior. I do believe God chooses people sometimes to do this work, but that they do have a choice. If a person chooses not to do what God is asking of them, God may then choose another to do that task. I also believe that even if you choose not to follow God's call to do something, it doesn't mean the "hounds" are called back. God still wants to help you to have a better life, or to be at least a little better in the life you have—and God will keep asking.

One of the biggest downfalls I see in the church is we want to bring logic where there is none, and we want to brainwash people or argue them into submission. We want to make them see things our way—God's way—and we are bound by rules that rely on our flawed human insight, which doesn't see into the heart of a person.

Sometimes the best form of evangelism is just to back off. Now wait. Before you throw this book across the room, hear me out. What we're trying to do in these situations of high resistance is really not ours to do. It's the Holy Spirit's work. Our job is to love people, walk with them, give them the Gospels, then love them some more. Those are the basics, and it's very hard to do just the basics when you see that someone has so much to lose. But it's important.

In the Name of Jesus

People get excited about Jesus, and sometimes in that excitement people do some mean, nasty, or strange things—all in the name of Jesus. As an old preacher friend of mine once said, "Sometimes people say and do things in the name of Jesus that would probably embarrass him to death." He's right. But why do well-intentioned people miss or misrepresent the teachings of Jesus so dramatically? While watching the *Dog Whisperer with Cesar Millan* one day on TV, a new parallel hit me: As Christians, we behave just like some of the more difficult dogs Millan tries to help. Like those angry, aggressive, confused—but otherwise good—dogs, we:

- don't understand who Jesus is
- get scared because someone speaks or acts against Jesus—like they'll hurt Jesus's feelings
- fight with and judge others to protect Jesus from sinful people
- think we have to be the pack leader so other people won't see Jesus *dying* for us as weakness

You may not think you are doing any of this, but actions speak louder than words. Stay with me here. When we get all amped up thinking we've got to protect Jesus, we're making *ourselves* the hero of every story. We're trying to become the savior, rather than allowing Jesus and the Holy Spirit to work through us. We're trying to be the hero, and that's not necessarily our job. While it's true that sometimes heroic actions are called for, more often we take on things we may not need to.

A Lamb on a Mission

What we have to remember when this kind of ego takes over is Jesus knew it was God's plan for him to die. Jesus *planned* to die. Everything he did, he did with intent. Jesus showed his immense power by giving himself to weak and feeble-minded people and allowing them to beat and kill him. Jesus, at any time, could have saved himself. He could have destroyed everything and everyone in his path. But Jesus isn't like that; it is not in his nature to do such things. Although Jesus *is* a warrior in waiting (don't take my word for it—read Revelation 14!), he embodies love, holding back justice.

Jesus submitted himself to God's plan with intent. No matter what happened unexpectedly, Jesus still worked the plan. Did things change? Did he have to adapt? Did he control every aspect as if those around him were God's chess pieces? All this is where the free will of being fully human comes in. It's clear that Jesus *did* allow people to surprise him; he *did* adapt.

Even though there were probably many times when things changed from what was expected, no matter what, God's plan would be done. The question for us is are we going to let God use us as God's agents on Earth, or are we going to respond the way Moses did when God first called him—by asking God to call someone else.

Here's the deal: As a leader, you have to first know how to follow. Otherwise, how are you going to know how followership works? How will people know how to follow you if you don't know how to follow the Holy Spirit? How can you know how to follow the Holy Spirit if you don't practice following?

Good questions to ponder.

Two Kinds of Following

It seems that there are two different types of following. One is following in power, with strength, and the other is following in weakness, with fear. We always have a choice. God designed it that way. We all have free will. When we choose to follow, we are following in power. By following Christ, we have even more options. We can still do anything we want to, but not everything will be good for us.

When we follow out of fear of what will happen if we don't follow, we are following in weakness. When we are afraid not to follow, we live in fear, waiting for the other shoe to drop. We feel like, and often are, victims. When things do go south—and they sometimes do, no matter who you are or how carefully you choose—you are alone. There is no comforter, no protector, no place to rest and regroup.

I submit myself to being a Christian because I know it will lead to a life with less stress, with a Savior who loves me who will send his Spirit to guide me when times are tough. So, as a Christian I have all the options everyone else has, but I also have the ability to go to a Savior for comfort and strength and the assurance that I am never alone.

You're Not Supposed to Be Luke Skywalker

I work with a lot of leaders, and after three decades or so of doing the intimate sort of work I do with churches, I identified a pattern that is so strong I gave it a name. Most if not all church leaders have a calling, a vision in their mind for this or that type of ministry they feel they are supposed to do. Many will say, "God put this on my heart to do" and they start out with every good intention. Then something happens. They start getting what I call the Luke Skywalker mentality—the hero mentality—like "I'm the hero of my own story. I need to do these things. God is *telling* me to do this . . ." Then they start adding to what God told them to do.

What they so often miss is that God may have said, "I need you to do this for a time" (and then perhaps, something else). What I see play out again and again are very sincere church leaders getting hold of a vision and then putting their own spin on it. ("I'm going to build it bigger and bigger and bigger . . . for God! . . . I'm the hero of this story! I'm the reason it's successful! God entrusted me to do this, and I am the new hero of the day in ministry!")

For some, all this bigger building may be necessary and true for a time, but for most, it's possible the vision should be built only to a certain point because there is someone greater coming who will need it as a stepping stone. You have to be okay with that.

I've seen people get so invested and attached to a specific vision or a ministry that even after it starts dying, due to its usefulness being done, they spend the rest of their lives trying to keep it going, rather than letting it go and following what God has next for them. If they could just let go of all the crowd noise of winning and being the hero, they could see that what they needed to accomplish is done. It's hard for some leaders to know when to let go and move on.

If you're a *Star Wars* buff, you'll get the Luke Skywalker reference. For the rest of you (spoiler alert!), in the 1977 movie *Star Wars: A New Hope* there's a scene at the end that really points to the thought process here. In this scene, a character identified as Red Leader attempts to destroy the Death Star (an Empire superweapon space station), but the blow fails.

Suppose you're someone—in this case Red Leader—who has worked all your life, been educated and battle-tested, and is experienced leading major attacks against the dark side. You feel confident that you are the one who will strike the blow that will cripple or destroy the evil Empire.

And somehow you miss.

But somewhere along the way your efforts encouraged a young fighter pilot like Luke Skywalker, and that encouragement is what set the stage for him to change the trajectory of the story.

Does this mean the young hotshot pilot is better than you—or more special to God? Of course not! He's just a young guy who's probably really scared because suddenly everything rides on him.

Maybe because of your encouragement, he has learned to listen. Maybe you helped him learn to stay open and trust the still, small voice within him that knows what to do. So, like Luke, when he hears that voice, he trusts the spirit within him and makes the move that changes everything.

This isn't to say that you did anything wrong; you just didn't get to be Luke Skywalker. Your role was to lead the team that set the stage for another to build upon.

Every church leader wants to be the Luke Skywalker in their ministry story, but most of them are actually the guy who goes ahead of the real hero. For most leaders, it will be your ministry that another person will build upon in ways you don't see and can't even imagine.

John the Baptist, the biblical figure most scholars agree baptized Jesus, knew this from the beginning of his ministry. He had his eyes opened to this early, so it was easier for him to accept the lesson we all must learn. He is a model of acceptance for today's leader. He worked with the attitude of, "I'm going to do great things, but I'm just a stepping stone for the person who will do even greater things. I'm happy doing the part I'm doing. It's that kid over there who will change the world."

What if your whole life's work is meant to give a word of encouragement on that one particular day to a child who will be our next president? What if your whole life is about one moment you spend that changes everything for the next Mahatma Gandhi? Are you okay with that? The trouble is we don't always—or usually ever—get to know the impact of all the individual moments of our ministries. So, why not assume that they each carry that potential?

What's interesting about church leaders over other types of leaders is you're going to do what you're asked by God to do. You're going to do it well, and to the best of your ability. You know that God will equip you to do it, and you really don't intend to take on more than what God wants you to take on. The trick is developing a razor-sharp awareness of where that finish line is for you, and accepting when you cross it that if you didn't get the job done to your own satisfaction, there must be a reason. Maybe that reason is the goal wasn't what you thought it was.

How do you navigate this challenge? How do you keep your ego in check and make sure you're still doing what God really wants you to do? Keep checking in and keep resting.

The Hero Trap

Ministry is filled with ego traps that well-intentioned leaders can fall into if they don't trust in what the Lord wants and what the Lord is doing. People take things on "for God" that can be the opposite of what God intends for them.

Even when I was in college, that used to drive me nuts. I studied both psychology and theology at a Christian college. A typical question we'd get from some professors was, "How many souls did you save this week?" Like notches in the belt, it was all about "winning souls," "filling God's Kingdom," or "saving sinners." The idea was that people would now be going to heaven because of my classmates and me! No! It's not about me, or about the other students in my class, or about you, either. We are not the ones doing the saving. That's the Holy Spirit's job.

Do I talk to people about my beliefs? Yes, if they ask me, I'm going to talk about whatever I need to talk about—and then it's the Holy Spirit's job from there. I know that many people I've talked to have later become Christians. Maybe this is because of a seed I planted, or maybe it's because of ground I prepared for the next person to plant, by loving on them, telling them their truth, and showing them something different. I'll never know, and I'm not supposed to. Everyone is called to do this and to follow God. That is our only job.

Whatever brings people to Christ, it's the Holy Spirit that makes it happen, pure and simple. The Holy Spirit works through me, and in them. We can't put more on ourselves than showing up. I may be good at talking people into things, but if the Holy Spirit isn't in it, that's just persuasion, *about* me and *for* me. That's me trying to be the hero.

So how do you stay out of the hero trap? Remember when you're talking to and leading people, that you may carry the shepherd's voice, but you are *not* the hero—and you've got to be okay with that. Say what needs to be said, firm and kind. Maybe you have to say and do things that are hard. That's part of your job. Things that are hard to hear must be said in love, and with encouragement, so the person you're talking to will want to do the work that needs to be done in order to get to the next level, whatever that may be.

Not every church leader is going to be rich, prosperous, healthy, and have a megachurch. Sometimes it's the smallest ministries that have the biggest impact, the places where you actually have the time and ability to reach into someone's life. You may just have ninety people in your church while the other guy has 30,000. That doesn't matter when you've had the time to breathe the Holy Spirit into the members of your parish. The other guy may not even know all the people in his.

Is either ministry good or bad? No. We all have our own path to follow and our own impact to make. The person leading the ninety is no better or worse than the person leading 30,000. They're different callings for different purposes. The church with the smaller congregation may include a person who will change the world and who *needs* the personal touch that church leader is uniquely qualified to provide. The church with the 30,000 may, because of its assets, be able to reach deep into an underserved segment of the population to empower someone there who could never have achieved their world-changing scientific discovery had they remained trapped in rural poverty.

Neither leader would likely ever know the ripple effect of their ministry, of following the single path God has laid out for them. That's why it's important to treat *every* person as someone who could be the one who changes the world as a result of your leadership, or someone who could influence someone else who then changes the world. When you start the domino effect of doing what is yours to do, no more and no less, you will set good into motion that will influence layers and layers of people—generations who don't even know you or why they do what they do. Remember that guy who flew ahead of Luke Skywalker.

Being part of the plan, learning to listen for God's voice, and following that voice with the full trust of sheep following their shepherd—so you can then lead others in that same voice—is the life you're here for. Trust me, it's going to be richer and more impactful than anything you can imagine on your own.

Do You Know What I Mean?

- When in your life or ministry have you experienced a *schmegge*? How did you respond? How would you respond now if the same thing happened today?

- Have you ever caught yourself trying to be Luke Skywalker, the hero of your own story? How did that realization come to you and what did you do about it?

- When you see others falling into the hero trap, what can you do to gently lead them out of this ravine and back to discovering the path God has laid out for them?

CHAPTER 3
Lead from Outside the Box

The point of all this pushing is not to be rebellious or hard to get along with—it's just a way of testing to see if what you may have assumed to be a box is really a box at all.

■

It had been a rough week of travel, meetings, installations, and problem-solving in churches with all kinds of unique challenges (don't they all have them?) and I was finding myself in need of rest. I needed renewal and time with God and nature. We had spent the past week in Los Angeles, California, and then worked our way through a series of jobs throughout the state, ending up in Sacramento. As I always try to do on these West Coast work trips, I rented a convertible for a drive up US Highway 1. (If you've ever driven that route, you know why. It is a breathtaking picture of God's creation!)

When I reached a particularly beautiful stretch, confirmed by the "scenic overlook" marker, I pulled off the road, and got out of the car. First, I just stood there and looked up and down the coastline. It was one of those super-clear visibility days and I could see the coast for quite a distance. I remember thinking how the last time I flew over this coastline it looked more or less like a straight line—from 30,000 feet above, thousands of miles of coastline makes the edge of this little part of the continent look fairly linear—but now, standing atop a steep embankment several hundred yards from the water's edge, looking up and down the coast as far as I could see, there were all sorts of interesting inlets and curves and irregularities to the shoreline, none of them visible from the airplane.

You know that picture we all carry in our minds of ourselves strolling, carefree, along a shoreline, listening to the waves crash beside us as we contemplate the universe and our own place in it? That was my thought as I scrambled down the embankment to walk that beautiful shoreline. It was still a few hours before my next meeting, so, I decided to take this time—as I so often advise others to do—to just rest, breathe, and be with God next to this magnificent shore.

Okay, well, that wasn't exactly my experience. Once I made it down the embankment, squinting back at where my car was parked and hoping I had remembered to lock it, I began my leisurely beach stroll. Except it wasn't so leisurely. There were bumps, rocks, jagged edges, and ups and downs to scale. That shoreline that had looked so smooth from the road was much more complicated than it appeared, and navigating it in the reality of my gritty wet shoes was a very different experience than gazing upon it from the scenic overlook.

It was then that I recognized another parallel to ministry and leadership. We tend to see things in a big-picture way only, like the whole coastline from an aerial view of 30,000 feet. It's from up here that we make judgments about people and situations, and we try to lead without really understanding the ins and outs of what's going on down at ground level—what's *really* happening in somebody's life. Making big-picture decisions without considering the street-level complexities can crush people. You can steamroll them without realizing it. It's easy to think something is clear-cut, in simple black and white, when in reality, it's shrouded in many different gray areas. The realization that people live in shades of gray can change everything.

As leaders, we need to have a vision that keeps the big picture in mind at all times. But when we look at a situation from *only* that 30,000-foot-above view, no matter how sharp our eyesight is, it's easy to miss the real topography—the people, dynamics, and circumstances—that complicate the landscape. While we may think we understand the situation fully, the on-the-ground reality can be quite different. When you climb down that embankment and slog through the weeds with the people involved, when you really get into the previously unseen parts of their lives with them, you begin to see that the situation is often a lot more complicated than it first may have seemed.

Going back to our shepherds, think of how they had to scan the terrain ahead of them in search of safe places for their sheep to walk, graze, and rest. Think about how the topography no doubt changed the closer they got to an area they thought would be safe. Think about the adjustments they had to make, sometimes on the fly, when things were not as they first appeared. Don't you imagine they were constantly watching for complications? Don't you bet they were more than familiar with finding U-turns, detours, and alternative routes once they found a barrier too difficult or dangerous to cross?

As leaders, the big picture is definitely not the only picture we need to see. Things are almost always more complicated than they first appear. Hold that thought for a moment while we talk about boundaries—and how boundaries set up the paradox of choice.

Outside the Box

I always hear people talk about "thinking outside the box" (or, more recently, "thinking outside the *proverbial* box"). Today "outside-the-box" is just another performance cliché. However, back when it was a relatively new expression, people probably stopped to question: "What's the box?" Let's talk about the original intent for even talking about that box. Much like dispelling the archaic notion that the world is flat, at some point people realized they could become trapped or confined by a set of rules or way of thinking—in a "box"— that was limiting, and sometimes not even real.

The big point I take from this is sometimes we imagine boundaries that don't actually exist. We make up rules for these boundaries that really aren't accurate or real. Then, upon running up against an imagined boundary, we learn that we can stick a toe over the edge and use our imagination to push it back a little—or a lot. We might discover that the boundary we imagine is really kind of bogus, and we might just do away with it entirely.

Here's an example I love, mainly because of the business I'm in: Remember those great big antennas everybody used to have on their roofs for TV and radio? At first, with the technology of that time, antennas needed to be this big to work. Even on your television set inside, you had this big, long thing with widespread arms. (Did you ever have to put aluminum foil on the end of the antenna to get better reception, or was that just at my house?)

Then, in the 1990s, a guy named Nathan Cohen was inspired by an earlier study of the infinity contained in a snowflake (specifically, the Koch Snowflake, which relates to fractal geometry—we'll touch on this in a different way shortly) and he figured out that if you bend an antenna, you can make it smaller, and it's still just as long and powerful. Cohen used this insight to create a more compact radio antenna using nothing more than wire and a pair of pliers. Today's antennae still use fractal technology to power huge reception capabilities in a minimal space.

What I'm getting at here is sometimes we think a big thing won't ever fit into the boundaries we'd give it and, because it *has* to be that big, it won't work in the space we have available for it. (This applies to ministries, programs, and even ideas!) Well, what if you think outside that box? What if you bend it a little—maybe even coil it up—and figure out a way to make it fit within those boundaries and still have the strength and reach of its larger iteration?

Living Outside the Box

At some point after pushing enough of those boundaries, real or imagined, some of us learn that we can actually *live* outside those boxes of our own creation. We can continue to push against the boundaries we may encounter on the way to our goals until we hit a true limit.

The point of all this pushing is not to be rebellious or hard to get along with—it's just a way of testing to see if what you may have assumed to be a box is really a box at all. (Perhaps it's really just a triangle, and when you reached one of its sides your mind made a box based on where you imagined the rest of the corners might be!) And maybe you keep pressing outward until you reach what *seems* like a wall, but then you turn back because you don't want to fail. It takes courage to allow yourself to actually hit real boundaries to find out where they truly are. In other words (and switching metaphors because I may have worn this one out), you're on the road to something you want to try or accomplish, and you hit a bump. So, you play it safe and stop, turn back, and return to your starting point. But maybe if you were to be able to rise up a few thousand feet and look at the big picture, you'd see that bump more in perspective—as a minimal hindrance rather than a stopping point.

Now there *are* actual boundaries that create the structure and definition of our lives. Some of these we know, and some we don't yet know. Some of the best-documented ones are, of course, listed in the Ten Commandments, but there are plenty of other boundaries in our society that are just as real, like traffic laws and IRS "guidelines." The Bible doesn't really mention some of the hard-and-fast, undeniable rules of nature, such as the boundaries of physics (which include the concepts of gravity, energy, force, and electricity), but we tend to consider them more seriously as solid parameters. ("This is clearly a wall, so I won't push on it or bang my head against it.")

When we see and know a boundary is real, we may add a partition here or there made up of our own belief or interpretation (dogma, perhaps), which may not be completely true. These partitions may be connected to the real boundary in our minds, but they are really an extension of our own making. Stay vigilant and push against a perceived boundary to make sure it's really part of the bigger structure. Sure, this kind of testing may still have consequences (remember those sheep that kept falling into the orchestra pit and getting tangled in wires?), but as long as we are willing to live with the consequences in exchange for finding new opportunities for growth, a choice is just a choice.

Here's the thing, though. Most people don't want to risk their life or safety; they want leaders to do that for them. They want soldiers to fight their wars as they cheer them on. Many also make decisions based on how they feel on a particular day, including the decision of if what you're doing is good or bad. When they get bored, they will move on to the next pasture.

People want leaders who will represent the minds of those they lead: the mind of the people. Depending on their convictions, they think, hope, or assume that their leader will have their best interest at heart and will somehow know all their thoughts and feelings. They expect a leader to know which boundaries to push and which to back away from. It is up to you to find and test the limits that make sense to you, knowing that you're never going to make everyone happy.

A Ministry of Fractals

But what is *the mind of the people*—and how can you know it? The best answer I have is that the mind of the people is a fractal. In fact, I believe all of life is a fractal that has been created by God to help us learn to find the structure and order within our own chaos. If you're not familiar with fractals, here's a quick dip into this mathematical dimension of creation. Fractals are the repeating, self-similar patterns found throughout nature. They are easy to see in things like ferns (each branch from the main stem of a frond looks exactly like the entire frond, but at a smaller scale) and nautilus seashells (each chamber of the shell is an exact replica of the preceding chamber, except getting smaller and smaller, going from large exterior chambers to the tiniest interior chambers). There's an entire field of scientific and mathematical study known as fractal geometry (caution: rabbit hole!) that examines irregular shapes in the fractal dimension to measure the complexity of these shapes.

A fractal is a self-similar geometric shape that is infinitely detailed (think snowflake viewed under a microscope) and is continuously repeating in a recurring pattern called a feedback loop. With this understanding, it's not too much of a leap to think of how these patterns found throughout the natural world might also be present in the human brain and thought processes.

Have you ever noticed repeating thoughts in your own mind? How moods, opinions, ideas, and trends tend to cycle? How habituated thought patterns and feedback loops have become integral to breakthroughs in cognitive therapy and behavior modification? These are not random things, and even in the most unique snowflakes, patterns are present. They exist everywhere, and this awareness can inform the perceptions and abilities of leaders who learn to respond rather than react. When there seems to be only one way to do things within the boundaries people perceive, it sometimes pays to look a little bit closer. Things are not always as they seem. Sometimes there is an underlying pattern just waiting to be discovered.

The Fractal Coastline

We already talked about how things are both more complicated and simpler than they seem. Sometimes we tend to see things in groupings and from a distance. (Isn't it easier to keep things in nice, tidy packages when we can observe a situation from a little ways away?) Now it's time to discuss making better judgment calls based on perceptions made from a distance.

Let's go back to the coastline of California. From a space-high view, the approximately 840-mile-long California coast appears to be a straight line. From a mile-high view, however, we see that there are inlets and curves that can't be seen from higher altitudes. What originally looked like a flat 840-mile-long edge is revealed to be 3,427 miles of irregular shoreline. From my perspective standing on the beach, I saw even more intricacies. With my face just inches above the shore, I might see just a few more rocks. You get the point.

Now let's look at the Grand Canyon. Looking at a map, you could draw a straight line along the canyon wall and say, "Well, it's about 277 miles long." But if you *walk* the length of that wall (with safety equipment, of course) you will see (and feel) that same Grand Canyon wall is a lot longer than your straight-line assessment. Your travels in, out, up, and down reveal many more miles of wall than you ever could have imagined.

As a leader, do you really care about how long that shoreline is? Does it matter that life is fractal to an infinite degree? No. Who can afford to get lost in those details? Nothing would get done from that inches-off-the-shore view! We would be *paralyzed* by all those details and choices. But I'm glad someone does feel the need to crawl down into that Grand Canyon crevasse. I'm grateful for the insights and benefits of the knowledge produced from those excursions, and I encourage the people who do them to continue pushing those boundaries if that is what God put in their heart to do, because these discoveries help me understand that things are both simpler and more complex than they seem. The infinitely small picture relates to the big picture and vice versa, so the job of a leader is to see and consider the realities of both, and not overly focus on either.

As it turns out, most of life is a judgment call. We talked about the hard-and-fast behavior boundaries created by God in the Ten Commandments, as well as the other hard-and-fast boundaries in Earth's design, known as the laws of physics. While violating either of these types of boundaries brings certain repercussions (as does violating boundaries of law in our society), our free will gives us opportunity to explore within the certainties of these boundaries to discover which are made, which are imagined, and which are absolute. We are free to fall down and get back up, fail or succeed, and eventually find the balance in our leadership that commits to the choices that create the box we will live and serve in, even if that takes some time.

It's also important to note that while fractals are about organization, faith is sometimes about working in chaos. Understanding this "sacred geometry" of fractals is all about finding, recognizing, and appreciating the order embedded in that chaos. Sometimes this requires an extra measure of faith and trust that time will reveal the intricate connections lying beneath the apparent disorder. Like the shepherds, we must learn to walk in faith, knowing that sometimes when we are feeling embroiled in chaos, we are too close to see the order and that, with time and distance, we may (or may not) be able to see the pattern.

Boundaries and Cracks

The point of all this chaos and geometry is learning to create leadership that lives outside the self-created box and inside the boundaries of faith. With good balance between these extremes—and trust that the Creator who made the Earth has a plan—you can avoid spending too much time pushing boundaries and falling into the cracks, and more time steering people and finding ways to reset things when they veer too far from the plan.

It's important to see that there is a balance between knowledge and faith there for you to find and maintain to make solid leadership decisions. Using this knowledge to engage the thinking, or "executive," side of your brain will move you closer to your faith-centered goals so you can achieve what God wants you to do. It's okay to get a little swallowed up in the details from time to time—they're what make up our knowledge of the boundaries we experience—but you must also limit and control how long you're going to stay in the muck of decision-making to keep from getting stuck in a crack.

Going back to our overarching sheep analogy, God sees the dangers in our path and creates the boundaries that will keep us safe and moving forward toward our goals—the green pastures of a contented life. What we see as the big picture is not always the big picture at all, but merely our perspective getting in our way. Almost everything is more complicated than it seems, from seashells to aircraft, and it is our faith that helps us navigate the distance between the big-picture thinking and fractal geometry underpinning all of life. Learn to be the observer who can toggle between the big picture and the details in order to reset your perspective in ways that find balanced and productive leadership solutions.

Do You Know What I Mean?

- What examples can you think of in your own ministry where you found yourself "boxed in" by boundaries that weren't actually real. Did you make them up to feel safe? How did you respond?

- When have boundaries been imposed on you by others who were also just making them up to feel safe? How did you respond?

- When in your ministry have you been able to hold both the big picture of your overall vision and the fractals of day-to-day ministry at the same time and in good balance? Sit with that memory and the feeling it brings. Remember it.

CHAPTER 4
Distill the Paradox

When love is the main driver, when love is the main goal, when love is the main solution, all other choices become less important, and the world becomes a better place.

■

Choice equals freedom, right? Short answer? Not always.

A study of this surprising paradox was conducted by graduate student Thomas Saltsman and Associate Professor of Psychology Mark Seery of the Department of Psychology at the University at Buffalo in New York. Published in the *Journal of Biological Psychology* in 2019, the study showed that despite the apparent increase in opportunity we see when we have a lot of choices, the need to choose creates a "paralyzing paradox," as the combination of perceptions—the high stakes of the decision and our own abilities—collide to contribute to our deep-seated fear of making the wrong choice. "We love having these choices," Seery notes, "but when we're actually faced with having to choose from among those countless options, the whole process goes south" (Quoted in Bert Gambini, "Study: Many choices seems promising until you actually have to choose," University at Buffalo News Center, June 13, 2019).

When we perceive a gulf between the stakes of a decision and our fear of making the wrong one, we often choose not to cross at all rather than find a new place to cross. Studies have shown that having more than three or four choices causes our stress level to rise.

According to the 2017 National Institutes of Health article, "Stress and Decision-Making: Effects on Valuation, Learning, and Risk-Taking" by Anthony J. Porcelli and Mauricio R. Delgado, this kind of rise in stress around decision-making actually influences our basic neural circuits involved in reward processing and learning, while also biasing our decisions towards habit and modulating our propensity to engage in risk-taking (Anthony J. Porcelli and Mauricio R. Delgado, "Stress and Decision-Making: Effects on Valuation, Learning, and Risk-Taking," National Institutes of Health, April 14, 2017).

Put simply, this means that when too many choices stress us out, our brain automatically reverts to more habitual choices and ways of thinking. In this more or less knee-jerk state, we are not as able to consider the greater reward that might come if we take the risk of a more novel choice or solution. We think inside the box.

Admittedly, Porcelli and Delgado's "Stress and Decision-Making" study goes on to say that this dicey relationship between stress and our cognitive computations "poses a particularly thorny methodological puzzle." Their research also suggests that chronic stress may not only increase our tendency toward habitual responses, but also diminish our mindfulness of our more goal-oriented possibilities. Porcelli and Delgado also contend that there is plenty of evidence to suggest that chronic stress and repeated stress-associated experiences (like leading a church, perhaps?) tend to consolidate into memories stored in our brain's hippocampus that can then direct our neural resources away from more "executive" thought process and toward our "salience networks" that enhance vigilance and fear.

Summing it up, the acute stress of too many choices can limit our ability to compare the value of the rewards on the other side of each potential choice and can short-circuit our brains from goal-directed to habit-based decision-making. If there isn't a habitual decision to make then we table it, defer it, and put it off to, well, maybe never. This cycle of stress and decision-making is not only ineffective and overwhelming, it hard-wires us to repeat it, which can lead to a life full of the frustrating feeling of doing what we always do and getting what we always get. Sometimes the long-term result of this cycle is some degree of self-destruction. Sometimes the result is a legacy of following the crowd and whatever trend is popular at the time.

In his keynote address presented at the Handheld Learning Conference in London in 2009, Malcolm McLaren, best known for promoting and managing punk rock and new wave bands, including the Sex Pistols and Adam and the Ants—and an early commercial architect of punk subculture who helped globalize hip-hop—called us a "karaoke culture" (Malcolm McLaren, "Reflections of Learning," Keynote presented at the Handheld Learning Conference, London, October 6, 2009. https://www.youtube.com/watch?v=E-wtmV0fAAg). The Japanese word *karaoke* means "empty orchestra," a lifeless musical form unencumbered by creativity and free of responsibility. Regardless of what you think of McLaren or his lifestyle, he makes a solid point that the false promises of instant success deny us opportunity for authentic creativity, and that messiness and failure are key to true learning. McLaren's meteoric success was no accident. It wasn't luck. Love him or hate him, his was a planned leadership move to create something, prompting the slogan on his headstone: "Better a spectacular failure, than a benign success."

I do think there are some boundaries that are best not pushed. I will stay away from the hard-and-fast rules like the Ten Commandments, or the reality of the Bible. I know many people who are pushing even these limits, changing theological doctrine based on how they feel about it. They are flying over the Grand Canyon, deciding the canyon is definitively this or that, when they've never been there to see it up close. They have never walked down the canyon's side or run their fingers on its walls to see it in its reality, forget the real deal at the microscopic, fractal level.

So, when the trusted people of God, the ones who stood on that holy ground, say that Earth was created in this way, and that Solomon was wise and we should listen to what he said, and that Moses led his people out of Egypt in a fantastic way, I say I was not there. I was not on that ground. I will trust that it was as it was said and, through faith, I will take the Word of the Bible and the ordination of the people who wrote it. Regardless of what I think, I believe that God will make the truth be known.

Faith, in general, is a choice. It's a big box with firm boundaries that, when we choose to live inside its parameters, feels safe.

Sometimes, if we want to feel even safer, we make a smaller box. When that starts feeling unsafe, an even smaller one.

It can be counterintuitive to the goals you have for your ministry or your team to create unnecessary boundaries and new faith systems and call it something it is not. This is where we sometimes have to stop and think about what we're doing and why. Sometimes we need to push those boundaries back out closer to the edges.

Belief Systems and Dogma

Belief systems and dogma can divide rather than unify. For example, take evolution and creationism. Evolution is the process where characteristics inherited by a species change gradually over time and new species develop from preexisting ones through successive generations. Creationism holds that the various forms of life were instantaneously created by God, usually the way described in the Bible in the book of Genesis. So often evolution is put squarely in the category of science and creationism is put squarely in the category of religion, but it seems to me that they are both faith-based beliefs. Both require faith.

I am fascinated by the concept that we were not created instantly by God, but in a more gradual process leading up to where and who we are today. So I understand it's a stretch for a non-believer to hear that something—God or a source energy or another cosmic force—took this planet and created the life it holds in a very short amount of time. Everything was designed so well and with so much detail that it was perfect and built to last, regenerating itself based on an infinite ecosystem that continuously regenerates, adapts, and feeds itself in a master plan that we are only starting to fully understand. (This is how deep fractal geometry really goes—from mountain range to snowflake, everything in creation is built upon fractals that are self-regenerating and self-replicating.) To a believer, the concept of evolution can sound a bit strange. However gradual, with so much continuous change, it seems that the natural world would have produced hybrid species—forms that got stuck somewhat in transition as each species morphed into something different.

However, if you look at history as a creationist, you will see something we don't understand and can't prove. God as the Creator had a design that used the material on the planet to put together the whole ecosystem set in motion at a certain time in history. Astrophysicist Fred

Hoyle is often quoted by creationists as having said during a 1982 radio lecture: "The probability of life originating on Earth is no greater than the chance that a hurricane, sweeping through a junkyard, might assemble a Boeing 747." Although this quote is often used in support of God creating perfect beings through divine action, Hoyle—an atheist and anti-theorist—was misquoted. During that 1982 radio lecture what he *actually* said was: "A junkyard contains all the bits and pieces of a Boeing 747, dismembered and in disarray. A whirlwind happens to blow through the yard. What is the chance that after its passage a fully assembled 747, ready to fly, will be found standing there?" (Fred Hoyle, *The Intelligent Universe* [New York: Holt, Rinehart, and Winston, 1984], 19).

At the end of the day, in both creationism and evolution the same materials were used, and the timeline to me is irrelevant—a miracle is a miracle is a miracle. So, to those who say God created *through* the laws of nature, and to those who say God created in a strict seven-day timeline as described in the book of Genesis, and to those who say God created as described in Genesis, but took millions of years to do it, and the "days" are metaphorical for billions of years, I say "stop muddying the waters." It is more about governing this body of life than the time spent to create it.

Many consider evolution fact. Many consider creationism fact. It takes more faith to believe one story over the other, and there lies the rub, but both require a degree of faith. None of us have the capacity to fully understand exactly, to the very smallest detail, how things were created on this large of a scale. We can so easily get pulled into camps that separate and divide. That's when dogma sets in, when we try to solidify, specify, and to define precisely. But the point is we need to stay away from the dogma, stay away from the gray areas that really do not matter. (Yes, you can argue about how much they do matter, but I say if they cause us to miss the main goal, then they don't. We have to focus.) The only thing that *really* matters is love.

Agree on love, and loving others as you are loved. Let's focus on that. If we focus on this main thing then we have a chance to take the confusion out of a very complex world, let alone theological debates. When love is the main driver, when love is the main goal, when love is the main solution, all other choices become less important, and the world becomes a better place.

Do You Know What I Mean?

- When in your life or ministry have you felt the most overwhelmed by too many choices? What did you do?

- When have you witnessed people you've empowered to lead getting caught up in the paralysis of analysis, missing the point of the choice they are making? How did you guide them out of that stuck place? How would you do that now?

- When you find yourself with too many choices, how do you reduce those choices to a smaller range? What helps you stay focused on the goal on the other side of the choice?

CHAPTER 5
Unpack How People Respond

*"There's a certain amount of training
shepherds do with sheep, and it should be exactly like
that with church leadership."*

∎

"This whole thing is just dumb."
I just can't believe it.
"They're not even listening to us."
Did you hear what he said when I spoke up?
"Nobody cares what we think."
I could tell by the look on her face she was zoned out.
"Do they expect us to go along with this like it's the greatest idea ever?"
They must think we're stupid.

I was sitting on an antique bench at the bottom of a stairwell in an old Gothic-style church, waiting to meet with leadership to determine the next steps for their new audiovisual (AV) system. I smiled to myself as I heard these sentiments, remembering being a teenager myself and having those same thoughts: Feeling like you know what's going on and how to get things done, and yet the adults, who don't have a clue, are calling all the shots. It's a helpless, frustrating, demoralizing, and sometimes infuriating feeling.

I could feel this conversation gathering steam every time someone new spoke up.

I wasn't sure what they were talking about—I was just catching enough to get the gist of the conversation. It was about programming or scheduling, or some new vision being handed down that wasn't sitting so well with them. I figured maybe they were teens grousing about their parents. The takeaway was somebody just didn't know how to get things done. Someone should not have said this or that. There was a clear feeling of "they just don't understand what we've been through."

To my surprise, when the group made its way down the stairs and out into the lobby, they weren't teenagers at all. Far from it. This was an older crowd. We're talking *retirees*. I laughed to myself as I relearned the timeless lesson that people are wired pretty much the same, whether they're children, corporate execs, or octogenarians. Once people learn a coping mechanism for emotional frustration, most tend to keep using that same method to deal with angst until they die—and it all sounds about the same. (I am not calling people sheep, but this does sort of align with the idea that we're all wired more or less the same way, and that emotions drive the primal reactions we have when we feel threatened, abandoned, neglected, or ignored by our peers and leaders. You can dress it up however you want to, but underneath all the exterior fluff, we're all pretty much the same.)

People who lead would do well to understand this reality, recognize what lies beneath the bluster of emotion, and learn how to keep relationships growing.

Creating a Shared Vision

A key point of leadership is knowing that how people respond to certain things has a lot to do with what they're used to doing—what they learned as a kid—and how that has evolved into what they've learned as adults. Sometimes it's also what society has told them to do.

You have a vision, and you know everything about it—what it is, where it came from, when it came about, why it is important, and how to make it happen. But leaders, especially new leaders just coming in, jump right to sharing that vision and expecting everyone to jump on board. The people you lead expect you to have a vision. They are looking for you to make the tough choices, so they don't have to. But they reserve the right to complain about it.

Let's say you come in with this great idea, a fully fleshed-out vision for what will be of great benefit for all involved. It will accomplish things everyone wants. It will solve problems. It is an answer you—and maybe an entire executive team—have worked on for months, maybe even years. Then you call your folks together and you say, "Hey, here's what we're going to do. It's going to be great! Come follow me, let's do this!"

The people respond, but not with the praise and adulation you were expecting. They immediately start grumping about it, often outside your presence or ability to address it directly.

> "Well, here's what he doesn't understand."
> "He doesn't know what he's doing."
> "Here's the problem."
> "Here's what's missing."
> "Has he even thought about [fill in the blank—ad infinitum!]."
> "Blah, blah, blah." (Baa, Baa Baa.)

What's easy to forget as a leader is that everyone comes from their own underpinning for how they are going to respond. Each has their own emotional foundation and unique life experiences acting as the gears that drive their reactions. All of these people together, the whole herd of them, may be similarly wired, but they're each thinking something different—and the more people you have, the deeper the fractal subculture of individual experiences. If you're not aware of this dynamic, the more you can get caught up and mired in the mess it creates.

Going back to our example of presenting your new vision, it really didn't matter how well you explained it, how on point your PowerPoint was, or how carefully you laid out your talking points. It was too much, too fast.

There's a certain amount of training shepherds do with sheep, and it should be exactly like that with church leadership. If you don't bring them into your vision and way of thinking—step-by-step onto the path you're leading them down—you can't expect them to understand and respond as you want them to.

Your task as shepherd is to help them understand. You want to help them connect with your thinking and learn the advantages of this new direction in order to encourage them to go the direction you're leading them. You want to help them become part of the bigger picture so they can identify and help with it, rather than dig in their heels with the attitude of "I just don't see it" or "this is dumb."

Sure, you can force it. There are ways you can *make* it happen, but that doesn't really teach anybody anything. From where I sit, I can see a better way.

The Disconnect

In my line of work, I observe and work very closely with the leaders of many different types of churches and other faith-based businesses who deal regularly with this issue of a presented vision receiving an unfavorable response. I've witnessed many levels of healthy and less-healthy scenarios across the board, but the one I'm going to focus on here is the one I see most. It's the one that always makes me want to cry.

These are the instances where there's a growing organization with a great team of people (who are not perfect, but have good hearts and a good variety of age and gender in their fold). The organization is seeing spiritual growth and lives changed, and its leadership is on fire with new ideas. Then (and this where the crying starts), the vision starts outpacing the followers. The leader starts controlling everything more and more tightly, while the parishioners are getting pushed aside in the name of "progress." Beloved pillars of the church are asked to leave because they question the new vision, and the leader begins to take over the decision-making at every level. The next thing you know, everyone is at odds. Battle lines are drawn, sides are chosen, and the once-united tribe—now divided over the vision—forgets why it is there in the first place.

Now you might say, "Well, that pastor has a problem," or "That's got to be an isolated incident." If only it were. I see it all the time. And every time the similarities are striking. This disconnect happens a lot, and in many different ways. It is not that you shouldn't push or shouldn't stretch. It is that you need to *teach people how* to be pushed and to stretch as you show them that you have their best interests at heart, too.

I heard something the other day that resonated with me on this exact thing. We asked one of our clients, "What do you get out of ministry?"

"Love," was the great answer.

Now, I know it may sound like an oversimplification, but in this context, it is profound. What we're all after is the all-encompassing love of God. It's not about you, it's not about me, it's not about us. It's all about God.

You can't keep a plant alive without watering it. You might be all about liking that plant, but if you don't properly care for it, it will die. Just like our children. If we don't properly care for them, feed them, clothe them, give them at least some affection, they will die. And if you don't feed and properly nurture this love within a faith community, the community will die. When the dynamic, vision, or leadership changes, the most important thing is not moving forward, but *staying planted* in the love that sustains you.

I attribute everything to layers of knowledge, and the tools that go with this layering are called wisdom. (So when I say "adolescent," it's not age-specific, but *wisdom*-specific.) Let's look at an "adolescent" situation, such as when a group of people, or a tribe, if you will (I think that's one of the best words to describe this close-knit, interdependent relationship grounded in God's love), is being guided in a new direction. As leaders we need to realize that in order to move forward, we first must help the members of this tribe grow in wisdom.

The disconnect comes when leaders don't understand the fundamentals of how people respond—and that they need to *grow the people into their vision* in order for them to see the beauty in this new path. Often, leaders think their job is to have the vision, to communicate the vision, and then after that, everyone is just supposed to fall in line. Once people know exactly what they're supposed to do and how it should be done, they'll just hop right up there and do it, right? No. That's not how it works. To have a vision catch on—and everyone work toward the goal like it was their own idea—takes a little more work to grow people into it.

As a father, I may have a vision for what my son needs to do to clean and organize his belongings. I can explain it clearly, step-by-step. I can paint a picture of the rosy results. I can even give him a checklist. I can "monitor" his progress—and yell and scream and stomp around—and it *still* will not get done the way I planned. It just won't.

So now I have a couple of options. I can make him do it again. . . and again. . . and maybe even again, until I think it's done correctly. This usually comes with a surprise later, when I open the wrong door, find everything shoved into a hiding space, and it all falls out. (You know what I'm talking about; you've seen it and have probably done it yourself!) The other option is to say, "Just forget it; I'll do it myself." This is frustration laced with self-righteousness, the idea of if you want something done right you've got to do it yourself.

Sometimes, if you have only limited time, or it's a one-time thing or whatever, you might be able to just get it done yourself and move on. But as a leader, this practice helps no one. What's worse, it's a trap.

I see good, growing churches break all the time when leaders get so wrapped up in tasks that they miss the opportunity to lead. They feel that they need to control every detail. They end up squeezing the life out of everything. There's a 1961 Looney Tunes cartoon of Hugo the Abominable Snowman grabbing Daffy Duck and saying, "I'm going to love him and hug him and squeeze him and never let him go," as Daffy's eyes are popping out of his head and he is trying to breathe and wriggle away. For some reason I always think of this cartoon when I see a church leader holding on too tightly to their vision because they love their vision too much.

I know of at least three churches going through this same thing at any given time—and I've been doing this work for a long time! Because I am working closely with both the pastors and the people on staff, it's easy for me to see both sides. I also know that there are three sides to every story: your side, their side, and the truth, which usually falls somewhere in between. These are healthy, growing churches that are doing very well, then the new vision comes along and the people are not prepared.

It's About the People, Not the Vision

Hear me out. The vision is important. It's why you're there. It's the legacy you will build in your community and *with* your community. But before you can get going on making that vision happen, you have to get right with the people involved. Bring them along. Make your vision their vision, too. But how do you do that when everyone is so set in the this-is-how-we've-always-done-it mentality?

One day a few years ago I was called to meet with a church that was expanding rapidly. They were going to build a new building and they wanted to consult with my group on their AV systems and installation. I thought this was going to be like a lot of the other churches we had been working with that were growing crazy fast—very sleek, high-gloss, and contemporary.

What I found when I arrived was just the opposite. This place looked like my Grandpa's church from the 1950s! What amazed me about it was this place was *packed*. They had multiple services, all full, every Sunday. This was a very traditional church, and one of the things the pastor wanted me to design for the new stage was sound-related: When he stomped to make a point, he wanted it to resonate throughout the building. But he also made statements like, "There will never be a drum on this stage while I'm here." It seemed the organ would reign supreme as God's main instrument of praise.

As I looked around, I saw a very elderly congregation, and when I began talking to members individually, I learned that many, if not most, were displaced from the churches they grew up in—churches that some of them had even started. When the popular wave of "new vision" came through town, everyone else in their home churches had wanted to change, and they were pushed out.

Now, you might say, "Well, you have to move past the 1950s if you are going to reach people in today's world," and I agree with that to some extent, but at what cost? Just as I don't think it's healthy to expect people to continue doing what they are used to forever, for people to suddenly get the ultimatum, "If you don't like it, then leave," is just as unhealthy for the church overall. When it becomes all about the vision and not about the people, you're heading into some rough waters.

There's a balance to find there, and it's your job to find it for the sake of the whole flock. Sheep don't know what they don't know; they depend on you, their shepherd, to set the pace and parameters for the path you will walk. Finding this delicate balance is hard work. Extremes can be deadly to your vision.

Consider the pendulum, a weight suspended from a fixed point so it can swing back and forth under the influence of gravity. You find this simple gravity-driven principle at work in things like metronomes, clocks, seismometers, and even amusement park rides. In this application of the pendulum principle, consider that the center point, when the weight is at rest, is always God.

Somehow in these situations of old versus new, this side versus that side, our job is to find that balance—and this is way more challenging in real life application than it is in engineering, for sure! Whether it's balancing your personal life (work-life balance) or balancing a push forward (old-new balance), extremes and polarized all-or-nothing thinking are easy traps to fall into. It's very easy to work on autopilot and avoid having to think critically or make any decisions of impact. The typical result is your vision can suffer a slow and painful death by committee.

Think about your own body. Some might say, "Give it everything it desires. If you crave it, it must be good; your body knows what it needs." Others might say, "Don't give in to your body's desires; in fact, stay away from anything that might taste or feel good, as it will lead to more sin."

In the "Eros" chapter of his book *The Four Loves*, C.S. Lewis quotes St. Francis of Assisi, a patron saint of animals and the environment who is known for referring to his body as "Brother Ass." "*Ass* is exquisitely right because no one in his senses can either revere or hate a donkey," Lewis writes. "It is a useful, sturdy, lazy, obstinate, patient, lovable and infuriating beast; deserving now the stick and now a carrot; both pathetically and absurdly beautiful. So the body" (C.S. Lewis, *The Four Loves* [New York: Harper Collins, 1960], 129-130).

Even though St. Francis was notoriously referring to how badly he treated his body, I love this quote because the sentiment is so true for me. Sometimes I need a kick to the butt and sometimes I just need a hug or an affirmation, but I need neither of these all the time. When people have too much of an extreme, they go from healthy to a form of dysfunction.

Finding the Balance

Balance will allow your vision to move forward as you intend, while honoring the people you lead—who all come from unique vantage points, life experiences, and personal baggage—and leaving no one behind. Sounds pretty simple, huh?

To begin to unpack this, let's first look at the idea of growing someone into a vision. Going back to the example of my son cleaning out and organizing his room, I need to help him understand exactly what I'm expecting from him and help him understand that this is part of how real life works. I will spend whatever time it takes to walk him though exactly what needs to be done and why; then I'll work to make sure everything I'm asking for and the reasoning behind it is clear, and let him know that shortcuts will only lead to double the work later.

What I'm doing here is less about teaching him to be a trash picker-upper and more about his playing a part in the whole vision of what his life would be like with clean and orderly surroundings. In this process he will see that we all have a part to play in our own well-being. Yes, the trash needs to get picked up and someone needs to do that. While this job may seem trivial, it is actually very important because, without it being done, none of the good stuff can happen, and the potential for smell, bug-and-rodent infestation, disease, and other bad things will escalate and destroy the overall vision of cleanliness and order.

At churches, I always talk about how different jobs are important. Sure, some jobs may *seem* more important, such as being the leader of worship, the music director, or the person teaching, but the weight of importance also needs to be put on the people filling other roles, such as the trash collectors, the greeters who welcome people when they arrive, those handling the childcare, those who communicate the details of what you're doing as a church, and the person making sure the live stream goes up on time. The importance of these positions needs to be understood and appreciated on a deeper level for the good of the whole.

Like my son with his room, people of a faith community need to be walked through the expectations, guided through the *why*, and provided with answers to their questions in order to do what is expected of them. People need more shepherding into a vision than "do it this way because I said so."

This is not because they have any real need to know. Sometimes an order is an order and we just need something to be done. But if you are trying to get true buy-in on your vision, people *do* need to know more. They need to understand the reasons for doing things in the way you are laying out, and they need to know that *they* are being taken care of, too.

Jesus sums up this idea when he talks about how we get back what we give to the world. God teaches us, through the church and through each other, to give this world mercy and lovingkindness. I think it applies to the natural, spiritual principle of interconnectedness, in which we live generously and graciously. In this "growing into" process, I think it means that if we are generous with time and information to create a deeper understanding of our vision, that generosity of spirit will return to us—and to our vision—measure for measure. Put simply, people will usually give only as much as they perceive they are getting.

The *perceive* part is where it can get tricky. Everyone has a different style, and everyone has different needs. Finding what it is about your vision that fills all these individual people up is a challenge you will need help with. You will also need to help them understand that Jesus is ultimately where we all must go for that filling. But you're going to need something deeper than just saying, "see Jesus."

When I talk to church leadership about taking the next step toward a new a vision, I try to start by considering the people they have, and discovering where they are emotionally in regard to the new vision. Most of the time I hear the same answers: The younger people in the congregation are open to moving toward a different way of doing things, and the older members of the congregation are holding fast to "the way we've always done it," and do not want to try new things.

Building a Shared Sense of Legacy

I've been in churches where they just say, "Well, this is what we're doing now, and if you don't like it, you can leave," and I'm totally okay with that if it's a new church that was started with that vision, and there's a specific demographic they're going for. But for the churches that have history—and people who have been part of its movement from the beginning—to say, "We are turning on a dime in a new direction and you are more than welcome to get off here," isn't the best idea.

The best leaders, from what I've observed and witnessed firsthand, are those who, first and foremost, spend some time just loving on their people, telling them how much they are appreciated, and getting them involved in all aspects of the church. Next, they talk about legacy, informally, one-on-one, in small groups, and sometimes in even larger town hall settings. There are crucial questions to ask here:

> What are we leaving behind for the next generations of this church?
> What are we doing to impact God's kingdom as a whole?
> Who are we teaching?
> What are we teaching?

All of this discussion tends to resonate with the older generation. And of course it does. They understand that the world is not the same place it once was, and that their time left in it is growing shorter. However, sometimes they are also the ones who need a little extra time to understand and get comfortable with the concepts that scaffold your vision.

Don't leave them behind! The older generations are *also* usually the ones with the experience and resources that can help you most. When I say "resources," most people puff up and say, "it's not about the money!" And I agree. The money side of resources is only a small part of what I'm talking about here. I'm talking more about the resources of time and experience. Who would be the best mentor for a younger person? Who better to talk about life with than a person who has seen it, lived it, made mistakes, and made it through?

I can tell you without hesitation that one of the best set of mentors for my son when he was between the ages of thirteen and sixteen was a group of retirees who just took a bit of time to talk with him regularly and started caring about him. Did they talk about deep stuff? Maybe, but probably not. Sometimes he went to them with questions about things they talked about among themselves. For sure there was a lot they did not understand about his life and what he was into with music and art, but I still see them light up when they see each other, and for those five to ten minutes, both sides still give and get a lot. The interesting thing is that they always talk to him as a man. They don't play around or act like he doesn't know anything, they get real with him—and he loves that! Sometimes they ask for *his* help with things, making my son feel like the expert. Put simply, they are filling each other up.

Now this is not a traditional style of mentorship; they've never spent hours formally together the way those involved in more traditional mentorships might. But through small interactions and experiences, these older people formed a real link to the younger generation, even if just casually. They are the ones who are most open to sacrificing their comfort in the status quo in order to see their church's increased reach into the world. This is what a lot of churches are throwing away because they don't know how to make changes without alienating people. Yes, it is tougher to do. It takes a lot longer. Despite your best efforts, you will still lose some people who are just in church to be comfortable. But many others (and some may surprise you) are looking for an opportunity to have meaning in their lives again.

I'll tell you, if you want a great experience talking about change with people, go to a retirement community and take a bus to bring the people who live there to church. Invite them to stay all day, feed them, take care of them, and listen to their stories. They are the best people to talk about change with. They can be of such great value to both church staff and congregation that some churches develop retirement homes and apartments right on their property. They understand the value of accessing the insights of this demographic and want those who belong to it to have easy access to the church.

One church I worked with has a very interesting way of accomplishing this objective of involving multiple generations in the evolving vision for its faith community. The church has multiple services and, on purpose, each has a different style. I know this is not unusual, but here's where the difference is: The church asks the people from each service to stay and serve as ushers and greeters at the next service.

So, the idea is to have the people attend the worship service and style that feeds them, and then to serve the church by staying for the next service to help. Be the greeters, be the coffee makers, be the huggers—whatever is needed—but be *involved*. Almost without exception, when individuals meet and greet the others who are coming, help them feel comfortable, and see that they are getting fed, too, they see a whole different picture of the legacy they're helping to create. Rather than just being told the facts, they have become part of the story. This is how to grow people into a vision. Sure, coordinating all that creates a lot of extra work for a lot of people, but suddenly everyone feels they are worth the effort. Everyone is now giving back, feeling good about it, meeting the vision and legacy face-to-face.

Most of the churches I've seen doing this gain buy-in from their people. Pretty soon everyone understands the vision on a fundamental level. They are on board with changes, and even if they don't love the music, or the style of worship all the time, they love the people; they love the tribe. The key is to develop their understanding and wisdom gradually, over time, until what they object to most is no longer objectionable at all.

There is an old myth that if you throw a frog in a pot of hot water it will jump out, but if you slowly increase the heat the frog won't notice. It's a problematic story on several counts we won't get into here, but, right or wrong, the idea is to make sure a steady heat is on to make a change, but not so much or so high that it gets overwhelming.

Connect with the Hope System

As we learn more and more about neurology, the branch of medicine concerned with the brain and nervous system, neuroscience researchers are tapping into a specific field known as neuroplasticity that ties behavioral neurology with communication strategies. In his 2023 article "The Neuroscience of Communication," Dr. Justin James Kennedy writes: "Leaders can harness neuroplasticity to enhance communication skills and create meaningful connections by understanding how the brain responds to various communication techniques" (Justin James Kennedy, Ph.D., D.Prof., "The Neuroscience of Communication: How the brain adapts to diverse styles," *Psychology Today*, October 10, 2023. https://www.psychologytoday.com/us/blog/brain-reboot/202310/the-neuroscience-of-communication).

Getting the messaging right in the area of generating congregational buy-in to your new vision (and the change it will create) means tapping into this field of research to develop communications strategies that do justice to both your vision and the people you serve.

This isn't about trickery—or using science to get what you want (that would be creepy). Instead, it's about working with the principles of behavioral neurology that are helping us begin to understand how people respond (to fear, primarily, which is what change represents for many), and moving alongside them to help create understanding and anticipation of good things to come. This helps to make people part of the successful implementation of your vision rather than members of the opposition, driven by a fear and dread of change.

Dr. Andrew Huberman, a neuroscientist and a professor of neurobiology and ophthalmology at the Stanford University School of Medicine, is the founder of the Huberman Lab, which researches brain function, brain plasticity, and brain regeneration. In a study with mice that focused on the midline thalamus, a mysterious area of the brain that has only recently been explored, Dr. Huberman found that stimulating this brain area converted a terrified, non-confrontational mouse into a mouse willing to confront its fears in a healthy and adaptive way. "It wasn't foolishly running into the jaws of a predator," he told Rich Roll on *The Rich Roll Podcast*, "but it was being very strategic in its confrontation." Dr. Huberman notes that the more interesting finding was if there was no fear stimulus, and that brain area was just tickled, animals—and he presumes humans—will work for that feeling more than for any other stimulation (Quoted in "Change Your Brain: Neuroscientist Dr. Andrew Huberman," Interview by Rich Roll, *The Rich Roll Podcast*, July 20, 2020. https://www.youtube.com/watch?v=SwQhKFMxmDY).

So why is this? It's due to dopamine, a neurotransmitter in the brain that plays a role in pleasure, motivation, and learning. Because these researchers were able to place tracers in the brain to measure connections, they found that the midline thalamus connects directly into the major hubs of dopamine released in the brain. The dopaminergic system (the release of the chemical dopamine in the brain) is the single reward system that underpins every single kind of reward a human being can seek—from food to sex to drugs to money to power (and more). Human studies going back to the 1960s (first published in the *Journal of Science*) confirm that given the option to stimulate a number of different brain areas, the subjects all preferred to stimulate the midline thalamus area.

Surprisingly, the feeling most associated with this brain stimulation was anticipation, and it tapped directly into the dopamine system that says, "something good is about to happen." Activating that state is not about acquiring the good thing, but rather it drives you forward in anticipation of it, which, as it turns out, is the most powerful form of positive reinforcement you can have. (Interesting, huh? Do you see where I'm going with this?)

In her 2021 book *Dopamine Nation*, Anna Lembke, a professor of psychiatry at Stanford University School of Medicine and chief of the Stanford Addiction Medicine Dual Diagnosis Clinic, calls this all-powerful reality "seeking," noting that it deals more with motivation, drive, and wanting, rather than getting or even taking pleasure in a reward.

So what does dopamine have to do with your vision—and more importantly, with sheep? (Isn't that why we're all here?) The link is this: How people respond matters to the success of your vision. For those who are resistant to change, regardless of what they express outwardly, it all boils down to fear. By taking the time to bring people into your vision, growing them into the legacy they can help create, and using this new understanding of behavioral neurology, you can change the trajectory of resistance. By crafting communication around your vision that meets people where they are now, you will help them understand where your vision wants to take them. If you can do this while tapping into their dopaminergic anticipation that "a good thing is about to happen," you will also activate a powerful internal drive—the "hope system"—in each of them. Who could imagine a more powerful engine of success? Wouldn't that be worth whatever time it takes to build it? Isn't that the ultimate expression of love?

Do You Know What I Mean?

- Think about a time in your ministry when passionate responses by the people you are leading got out of hand. How did you manage that?

- What would you do differently, knowing what you know now about that situation?

- What would you do differently had you recognized that the response may have been their coping mechanism, not a critique of your leadership or you personally?

CHAPTER 6
Reevaluate "Scary People"

*"As I look around at the people I know who are
the most grateful to God for the relationship,
I see the ones who have been forgiven the most."*

■

A long time ago I had a friend named Chris. I was not a Christian when I met him, but we were friends long enough that he would see that transformation in my life. Chris was an intimidating guy—about 6'7" and in great shape. He was a fighter who ran with the Black Panthers of the area. I had just gotten beaten up in a race riot up the street from his house when I met him.

I had known Chris for a bit, but when I sold my soul to Jesus, things changed. Suddenly I wanted to get to know my friend in a different way. Up to this point I had not cared about his family—or him for that matter—as, up to this point, I had looked at pretty much everyone just to see what I could get out of them. But Jesus had showed me a new way, and after a while I asked Chris if we could hang out. "I'd like to meet your family," I told him. It had taken some time for me to work up to that question, once we became *real* friends. So, I met his family and got to know them. He would ask me to stop over and see the kids. (He said they loved the "crazy white guy that had hair like a girl.")

For a long time I hadn't said anything about my faith. Instead, I asked Chris, who was Muslim, about his own beliefs. I had him walk me through how it all works in his mind. I was genuinely interested, and that seemed to make him want to tell me more.

One day after we had become pretty close as true friends, we were sitting in his living room, and I felt the Holy Spirit give me something to say (and this is what I still use to this day). "Chris," I said, "can you do something for me? I would like to sit with you and explain to you how my life has changed. I only ask that you do this for me because I feel like if I don't tell you, it is my fault, and I will be responsible. Whether you want to listen is up to you. So, just for my sake, will you do me this honor? After you do this for me, I will not bring it up again unless you ask me to." He looked at me for a moment and then said, "Sure, David, I'd love to hear what you believe."

So, I took him through the whole deal. Adam and Eve. Noah, Abraham, and the split of nations. Then on to the Christ that fulfilled the law, or "the embodiment of knowledge and truth" that instructs, as it says in the second chapter of Romans. Chris listened, asked questions, and seemed genuinely interested "for my sake." It was a good talk, and I went home feeling like I had done what I was asked to do.

Shortly after that conversation, I learned that a *schmegge* happened to Chris (remember, that's when you lean back a little too far in your chair and cross the tipping point of no return). He got busted for transporting drugs over state lines. While he was on bail awaiting trial, he found out his mom was in an altercation, so he went to her house to help her. Long story short, Chris beat up five police officers on the scene before their backup arrived and subdued him. The last time I saw him was when I went to see him before he left our local courthouse. As I was preparing to leave, he asked, "Will you please pray for me?" Chris was about to do time in Jersey State Prison, one of the toughest in the country.

Fast forward a few years. I had lost touch with Chris's wife and had no idea how to reach his family. One day I was walking through a mall, and I heard, "Dave? Is that you?" This was about three years later. I had cut my hair short and was in college. The voice belonged to Chris's wife, who somehow recognized me. "Chris was just asking me to try and find you!" she said. "He wanted me to tell you one thing: 'You were right.'"

After talking to her for a little bit, it seemed that after the death of his friend from some awful things that went on in prison, Chris gave his life to Jesus. "David, he is different," she said. "Not like the different that happened when he first went in, but different in a new and wonderful way!" I was blown away at how God had used that seed planted years ago to start growing a beautiful tree that I'm sure will do great things.

What does this story have to do with your ministry? Well, I'll tell you. We have to understand the value—and know what to do with—"scary people," those who may be considered "scary" because of their lifestyle, choices, or risky behavior. There are different types of scary people in the world. Many of them are just misunderstood, but harmless. Some are genuinely scary in the fullest sense of the word.

But the idea of scary people got me thinking. What makes someone scary? Is it the idea that they might take something that I cherish, or make it difficult for me to live and do things in the way I'm used to doing them?

In any society, the true scary people are those with nothing to lose, and those who believe they have nothing to lose. This type of person is free from all the things that normally keep people in line. They figure that the only thing someone can do to them is take the life they have—and they don't really like that life, anyway—so they do whatever they think will get them a better life or at least dull the pain of this one. Jail could even be a good thing, because at least they would get a meal and a place to sleep.

These people are all around us. Their perception is that life is not worth living. They can do whatever they want to and the worst possible consequences are still going to be better than what they have, so they are fine with either outcome.

I've always told my son that he has two choices: Control yourself or be controlled. Neither is pleasant, but at least with one you have some sort of choice about what happens. With the other, you give up any rights you have.

Freedom Is a Fairy Tale

Because we live in a fallen world, everything we do has consequences, either physically or spiritually (or both). Freedom, true freedom, is a fairy tale. All this freedom we think we have is great, and it is nice to have, but it is not true freedom. The only true freedom anyone can have is God's forgiveness.

"Freedom" as we know it, is less *actual* freedom and more of a way through which people are controlled. Sometimes we even feel entitled by our *perception* of freedom.

There have always been two main ways of controlling people: through physical or mental intimidation, and through fear of loss. Intimidation though mental or physical means is simply forcing people to do what you want them to do (usually either through fear of brute force, or threatening that if they do or don't do as they're told, something bad will happen to them or their family). People who are held down or oppressed into submission in this way can get to the point where they don't have any way to fight back. Some people get so beaten down they feel they have nothing to lose and they rebel. We've seen this played out in a lot of different ways throughout history. This is not a good or bad thing. It just is.

The second main method of control is instilling in someone the fear of loss. This is similar to the first method, but a little different. This form of control threatens that a person will lose certain freedoms they value if they don't abide by a certain set of rules. This manner of control always assumes that a person has something to lose, and that this thing has value to the person—it's something they feel is important or hold dear. This can be any number of things, from money, to reputation, to power, to sex, to drugs. (Often they are things that bring about a physical reaction.) The conundrum here is that control through loss means you need to make sure people feel that they are the ones in control of their decisions about what they do in life. That there is a clear expectation of cause and effect. For example, if I make the choice to work hard that I will make more money and live a happier life.

Many institutions in society try to control people through fear, including governmental and judicial systems, which have been set up to provide structure and stability. Scary people, those with less to lose, are more immune to this control. However, those in the middle class, raised on promises of prosperity, are more vulnerable. They are people with more to lose. If, through these controls, the middle class is squeezed or pushed too hard, if the middle class were to shrink substantially (or even disappear entirely), these people would begin to feel desperate. They might start doing things they wouldn't normally do, because they've become stuck in a cycle of perpetually feeling they have less and less to lose. If they ultimately become people who've lost it all, they may join forces with those who've never had it, but want it.

How would a population that has become increasingly desperate to meet its needs, with little to no fear of any long-term consequences for its actions, be controlled? It wouldn't. It can't be controlled. And when you have a population with a large percentage of people who feel they have very little or nothing to lose, you start getting what we've been experiencing in this country: riots, mass shootings, and other crazy things. What's the worst that can happen when you have nothing left to lose?

"One Nation, Under God"

Although the U.S. Constitution supports a separation of church and state, our forefathers baked God solidly into the formation of this country. I think leaders of today could learn a few things by walking back through this process and the forethought woven into it. God appears in the Declaration of Independence, in the Pledge of Allegiance, and on U.S. currency. The phrase "so help me God" has long been included in oaths and is still used in some official capacities today, as a way to show that a person *really* means what they say. I believe that embracing God as our forefathers did is a promising design for a stable country.

The framers of the U.S. Constitution knew the power of religion and faith. Although the United States was founded on freedoms, including the freedom of religion (a concept included in the First Amendment of the Constitution: "Congress shall make no law respecting an establishment of religion, or prohibiting the free exercise thereof"), the power of religion was so great, and religious devotion was so entrenched in everyday society, that both those who *wanted* the young U.S. government to give faith a larger role and those who *feared* it would have a larger role wanted religion explicitly addressed in the nation's laws. So it was: The First Amendment to the Constitution was adopted by the First Federal Congress in September 1789 and ratified by the required number of states in December 1791. ("Religion and the Founding of the American Republic: Religion and the Federal Government, Part 1," The Library of Congress, https://www.loc.gov/exhibits/religion/rel06.html).

"Too Good to Be Bad, But Too Bad to Be Good"

In modern society, when people have control over their decisions, they have "freedom," but if they don't live up to the standards of the law, they risk having everything taken away. Most people don't want to risk that, so they play it safe, doing what they need to do to pass scrutiny. They may break small laws, ones they think won't put what they perceive as the better things in life in jeopardy; they create their own limits. They are, as my friend Bill says, "too good to be bad, but too bad to be good." They feel that some smaller things are worth the risk, but that others are definitely not. Maybe they wouldn't rob a bank or kill someone for just looking at them the wrong way, but maybe they *would* speed on the highway, cheat on a test, or lie under the guise of being helpful.

All this is to say that in biblical times, the majority of people lived under "God's law," which was much more powerful than the laws created by the people. People answered first and foremost to a higher power, with the understanding that while other people here on Earth could harm or even kill you, God has you for all eternity. Gradually, over time, early governments started using and incorporating religious ideology into their own modes of control. They added bits of biblical truth to their non-biblical agendas as it served their purposes. The more governments got involved in God's business, the more the atrocities that grew out of this meddling came to the forefront—all in the name of God.

A Cycle of Splitting

The old tension between church and state has endured. In many cases, when the church did not conform to the government's wishes, it resulted in a cycle of splitting. Some governments absorbed the role of the church to a degree, assuming the role and function of God. The concept of God and life after death, however, were not applied: The judgment after death and the eternal life of souls were not factored in. The promise for adherence was not eternal life and salvation, but instead freedom from a fate determined and given by the judicial system: jail, or capital punishment. Fear of losing freedoms backfires when people truly feel they have nothing left to lose because they figure the worst that can happen is they are locked away (jail), but get three meals a day and a roof over their head, or they are sentenced to die (capital punishment) and get put out of their misery.

In his book *God & Empire: Jesus Against Rome, Then and Now*, Catholic theologian and prominent New Testament scholar John Dominick Crossan compares the modern-day United States to the first-century Roman Empire—and contrasts these similar histories (civil war; the quest for global dominance; and political leaders increasingly ignoring international law, disregarding the concerns of allies, and lifting limitations on military use) with Jesus's message of nonviolence. Through this lens, Crossan reveals "Pilate's Kingdom of Rome as violent repression and Jesus's Kingdom of God as nonviolent resistance," adding: "Beneath the problem of empire is the problem of justice, but beneath the problem of justice is the problem of violence" (John Dominick Crossan, *God & Empire: Jesus Against Rome, Then and Now* [New York: Harper Collins, 2007], 5).

In his article "8 Reasons Why Rome Fell," author Evan Andrews writes: "Constant wars and overspending had significantly lightened imperial coffers, and oppressive taxation and inflation had widened the gap between rich and poor" (Evan Andrews, "8 Reason Why Rome Fell: Find out why one of history's most legendary empires finally came crashing down," History, January 14, 2014; Updated September 5, 2023. https://www.history.com/news/8-reasons-why-rome-fell). Looking at today's current events and stressors in the Unites States, we could be on a similar (if not the same) trajectory, one that has been repeated over and over throughout history.

Rome took religion out of its government and created the "nanny state," a government that tries to give too much advice or make too many laws about how people should live their lives. Once a center for culture and innovation and prosperity, Rome became overindulgent. It stopped really making anything, choosing instead to import things and people to do all the work. The Roman government was focused on doing whatever it could to pacify the Roman citizens in order to get their votes. The parallels to today's United States are clear.

Today's Shepherd Wields New Power

When we try to take God out of government, the bottom line is it becomes more about politics than people. Many times, these politicized and polarizing "issues" are more about trying to get re-elected or trying to control the masses through rhetoric and manipulation than they are about true public service. While the scale and times are different, history suggests that the general outcome could be the same as the one met by the Roman Empire. In the end, the result will likely not be what the government intended at all, nor will it be in the best interests of the people.

It is incumbent on the church and faith leaders of today to remember that "empire" has a tendency to emerge in human institutions unless we are aware of and willing to understand our commitment to justice rather than power structures. To break this cycle of splitting, the new leaders must join forces *under God*, doing everything they can to shepherd solutions that remove this iconic power struggle from political arenas and to focus instead on the greater good. By working together to bring about the balance Jesus prescribed, faith and political leaders could create a system that actually serves the people rather than a political agenda. With this unified intent to serve humanity's higher purpose as described by Jesus, today's leaders could ultimately fulfill the promise of "one nation, under God" that our forefathers envisioned. Now *that* would be revolutionary!

Why I Love People with Nothing to Lose
Why do I love people with nothing to lose? They are the ones who change the world! If you look at history, most of the biggest changes were brought about by people who had nowhere to go but up. They hit bottom, but still had a passion burning within them to effect change. As I look around at the people I know who are the most grateful to God for the relationship, I see the ones who have been forgiven the most.

Look at Saul, who later became known as the apostle Paul. Talk about a scary person! This guy was the real deal, living a very scary life on both sides of his conversion. Before his conversion, he was a killer of Christians; after his conversion, he was one of the most courageous, in-your-face preachers the world has ever known. Even when he was beaten and persecuted for his Christian faith, he felt honored because of what he had been forgiven for.

I know some people think the most exciting things come from youth, and I wonder if this is because most of the time, young people, too, have nothing to lose! They are just starting the rat race, they don't yet have all the fear of loss we grow into by adulthood. They are fine with living out of cars and eating instant noodles. They will do what it takes to make a difference. When they are backed by good, positive mentors and resources, they can be very scary people—in a good way! They can be daring, savvy, influential, effective, and have reach!

Turning this idea of scary people on its head a bit brings us to this point: When we look at ourselves honestly, we each must ask, "Am *I* a scary person?" What does it mean to be a scary person in this context? Aren't we all called to be at least a little bit scary? In these terms, scary people are people who have nothing to lose *and* are hyperfocused on what they want.

Personally, my answer is no, I'm not even close to scary. I've *been* scary a few times in my youth—in a bad way for years and then, once God got hold of me, in a very good way. I had some interesting friends back then. (Remember my earlier story, when I was held at gunpoint and handcuffed because I was at a friend's house to take him to a concert at my church on the night his apartment got raided by police?) Unfortunately—or maybe *fortunately,* because I lived through them and became the better kind of scary—I have many more stories about things I now look back on and say, "What was I thinking!?"

Taking the "No Fault" Approach

When remembering those old scary days, I think about my ministry philosophy that came out of them: "It's my fault if I don't say it; It's your fault if you don't listen." Continuing to love on people even when they rejected my message broke down barriers that had been up for so long. I still have people I haven't seen for years come up to me and say, "Remember that time when you said it was your fault if you didn't say it? That stuck with me—you didn't judge me, and I was a real mess. You just loved me, and I never forgot that time you explained things to me."

One guy from my time as a nightclub bouncer came back to me and said that very same thing—and I came to find out, all these years later, he is now a Messianic Jewish rabbi! After reminding me of our conversation years before, he simply said, "Thank you for not pushing me away."

Nowadays, at the risk of mixing metaphors, I feel like a lion at the zoo. I look like I *could* be scary, but most of the time I just lay around and get fed. I don't hunt—I don't know if I could anymore. In fact, given a chance to escape, I would probably walk around a bit until dinnertime and then go back into the cage. Why? If I'm being honest, I'm content. I've worked hard to get the few things I have. I have little influence in the big picture of things, but I'm not starving. I have a bed, a car, a family, and I don't want to give that life up.

If I was asked to do so by God, I'm not sure of my answer. I would like to believe that I would rise to the occasion and say, "Yes! Here I am, Lord! I'll do it!" But in reality, I'm a little bit old and a little bit lazy (or at least that is the excuse I'm using today). Still, something in me longs for something more—part of me still wants to be the lion out of the cage, that free spirit roaming the countryside, spreading the message.

Here's the point: The choices we are making today lead us down one path or another. If forward movement is what I'm looking for, as much as I can muster, I need to get myself in shape to "run with patience the race that is set before [me]," as it says in Hebrews 12.

How to Get Scary

What about you? As you read this, are you identifying more with someone who has nothing to lose, more with the lazy lion ready to get out of that cage and do something meaningful, or more with the contented lion happy to stick to the cage? If you could do anything, what would you do?

Unless you are hearing a call from God to do something specific, and you have the opportunity already lined up, you'd best get to the gym to prepare yourself. I'm talking about God's gym, the one that leads you to the training you will need to do the work God will have for you.

Even in the best of circumstances, doing God's work takes diligent preparation. (Look at Jesus. He spent years trying to prepare the disciples, and some of them still didn't get it right!) So don't think you're going to jump in tomorrow and go full force, or you could break a hip or something. However, once you begin training and getting stronger—and clarifying the mission in your mind—you will start to become a scary person in all the best ways.

Do we have to drop everything and follow Jesus? Must we go from rich to poor? Is it really necessary to give it all away and only keep the clothes on our back to move forward? These are questions only God can answer. I'm not Jesus, I'll leave these things to him. But I can tell you that nothing in this world is cheap, and in order for the people who do take that extreme call, the scariest people, I want to make sure they have everything that they need to fulfill their mission.

I believe people are called to different things in different ways. I believe that a person who is good at business and makes millions of dollars can do better staying where they are—and if they want to be scary, too, they can use the money they make to support the people God puts in their lives who are supposed to be on the ground—the front line.

Imagine being a person who has lived a very simple life suddenly being given the money to support a mission that is really helping people. Because of this unexpected support, you are suddenly able to live the Gospels every day on a much larger scale. Both kinds of scary people are necessary to make these scenarios happen. One is no more important than the other.

In the Club—or On a Mission?

When we each look at our own motivation, do we *really* believe—or do we just say we do so we can be part of the club? If we're really being honest, are we doing our best for the mission, or the least we can get by with to remain part of the club? I used to be in *love* with Jesus—and then life started getting in the way.

I used to wake up excited about starting my day spending time with Jesus in scripture. I would miss just about anything before I'd miss spending that time with Jesus. I knew that if I didn't, my life would show it. At first, it wasn't a matter of "I have to make time for Jesus." It was more that I had to make time for other things—work, friends, or TV—because the only thing I was about was Jesus.

You see the paradox there. Sometimes we run around thinking we need to find a plan for our ministry that Jesus will like so he will bless our plan. Once we have that plan, it's ours to control. We can feed it until the plan or mission itself becomes more important than Jesus. All of a sudden, we realize we have missed Jesus's point completely. We've just been stressing out and living in the rat race.

I see this happen all the time with the pastors and church leaders I work with. They start out with the right set of goals of growing a church or organization into something special for Jesus. And then at some point it turns out that even though they built it for Jesus, Jesus has no real say in it. They still love Jesus, just like I do, but once they start to worry about keeping up appearances, keeping people happy, and making choices based on popular demand rather than where Jesus is leading, they're suddenly that caged lion again—and the cage is a nice, comfy building with a dependable salary.

Eventually, we start to remember with passion the days when we were running free, following Jesus at every whim, and seeing miracles happen in people's lives. Somewhere along the way we built a cage and set up mechanisms for timed feedings and a public that comes in to throw money at lions that once were amazing—and scary.

Yes, I know this seems cynical of ministry, but stay with me. The point I'm trying to make is that the goal you start with, when your heart is pure, is to do Jesus's work. All you want is to be with Jesus and follow him and do the work he asks to you do. Then at some point you stop doing things *with* Jesus and start doing things *for* Jesus—and that leads to the trap of people-pleasing.

To be free again would mean that you would have nothing to lose, and to have nothing to lose would mean that you are not working from *your* agenda but from *Jesus's* agenda, which is the hardest thing I've ever set out to do in my life. I'm no expert here (I've painted myself into this corner many times), but most people don't see this cycle for what it really is. When you do things for Jesus, in the name of Jesus, while pushing your own agenda, it's the opposite of faith and the destroyer of ministries. It's pride.

If you ever stare into the eyes of someone who only has one mission in life and has nothing to lose, someone who would stop at nothing, even death, would you be scared? I would only be scared if that mission would take more from me than I am prepared to give, or if it runs counter to what I believe to be true. In that instance, what would I be truly scared for, my rights or my beliefs? That's a trick question. No one can take your beliefs, so it always comes down to your comfort and your perceived freedom.

Do You Know What I Mean?

- When in your ministry have you encountered "scary people" — people with nothing to lose? How did God use that experience for good? How did that experience change you?

- Do you personally identify more with someone who has nothing to lose—or with the lazy lion ready to get out of that cage and do something meaningful? If you could do anything, what would you do?

- What have you done in your ministry to get yourself and your flock prepared in "God's gym" to train for the work God has for you and your organization to do?

CHAPTER 7
Crystalize Intent

The perception of how something looks, feels, or sounds has a direct connection to people's emotional experience of it.

■

Lots of people have ideas, but no real intent behind them. Or they have intent with no idea how to get there. Intent is more powerful than you might think. Intent without a specific plan is usually worse than having no intent at all. (Ever hear the expression "ready, fire, aim!" to describe this?) Sometimes we can have an intention that's partially formed, but nothing exact or specific. We have just a loosely held idea of what it is, and we're waiting for the Holy Spirit to move us toward something more concrete. This sounds similar to (but is different from) having an idea without any real intention (vague or otherwise) behind it and proceeding without first pinning down the intention for doing what we're doing.

    I know it may seem like I'm talking out of both sides of my mouth here, but the bottom line is this: It takes a clear vision to lead anyone anywhere, but clarity of vision will only take you so far. Intent is what *powers* vision. Once your intent is established (even if it's held somewhat loosely) and your vision is clear, then it's time to start generating the ideas that will evolve into a plan you and your church can accomplish. If you miss one of these steps, what you have is a bunch of people with some idea of where you're going but no clue how or why you're trying to get there.

Going back to our shepherd and sheep analogy, it's as if you know you need to find a nice green pasture, and all the sheep know is that they're hungry. If you don't have an idea of which pasture you want to get them to safely and why that choice aligns with your intent (keeping them safe from predators, for example), and you don't have a trail mapped out to get there—through the woods, across the ravine, and down the stream—the resulting communication with them will devolve into chaos. There will likely be lots of darting and bleating, with sheep making desperate moves trying to meet their own needs, because they aren't sure you're paying attention to them!

So, let's walk together through this complicated field of traveling with intent.

Know Your Flock

Before you can start aligning your intent, ideas, and action items, you've first got to be sure you know your sheep—or at least know who lives in the area you are hoping to reach. You might already have the intent (I want to plant a church!), but before you start designing logos and laying cornerstones, you have to figure out the demographics.

Who are you trying to reach? What is their experience of church or religion so far? How will you reach them? What will you try to reach them with? What do you want to empower them to do? It's crucial to discover and understand some important details about the people you want to serve—and empower to serve others. What are their needs? What makes them do the things they do? What moves them in the direction their community is driven? How are you going to be relevant in that community?

The Secret Language

Let's think about how we talk, the language only people familiar with Christianity speak. (Some call this "insider language.") Think about it from the perspective of the uninitiated. If you've never darkened the door of a church or been around people who have, some of the words and concepts we toss about without context can sound very strange:

> "The blood of the lamb" (Animal sacrifice?)
> "The blood of Christ washing over me" (Human sacrifice?)
> "Eat my body, drink my blood." (Cannibals? Vampires?)

Even the symbol of Christianity, the cross, was a terribly cruel torture and execution device. (Yet we wear it around our necks?)

If a person happens to come to church on a Communion Sunday, and we're talking about eating flesh and drinking blood, it has to be a little concerning, to say the least. I know these things are very important to our faith, and we are commanded to do them, but we do need to make sure that we put things in context for those who are new to church.

The conundrum of our times is if we are to preach the Gospels as commanded, we still have to figure out how to speak to the general public in ways that are easier to understand in the context of our culture. When we know our demographic, we can figure out how to communicate in the style most relevant to the people we are hoping to serve without watering down the message.

Offensive is an understatement when you think about the way the uninitiated, "unchurched" world might view our messages. Some of that is okay—some of it is supposed to be a hard pill to swallow; Christian life comes with challenges and some of them are hard— but that's more advanced stuff, not something to contend with the first day you walk through the doors of a church. Think about it. If you have never been around the Bible or heard about any of these things, the bar is pretty high for understanding most of what church people are talking about. There are a lot of ways we describe celebrations, observances, and traditions that we don't even think about because they're familiar. We've always said and done it that way. Sometimes we don't even know why!

I heard someone speak once about the Amish, the descendants of the strict Mennonite sect who settled in the United States primarily in the eighteenth century. It's interesting to me that they believe God told them any technology developed after the year 1850 is from the devil and off-limits. I know that sounds extreme, but if you look and listen to what some people say about change in the church, there may be a different cutoff date, but the feeling is pretty much the same.

So, what things should we lead with to bring non-church people in? If our intent is to have new people come into the full understanding of our faith, all those things about the body and blood and sacrifice of Christ are the most important things of all, but people can't learn and grow into that if they won't even come in the door. Should we just limit our reach to people who have, at the very least, been to church when they were young and know a few basic things about Christianity? Of course not!

Perception Is Reality

Over the course of my career working with church and faith communities of all sizes, and speaking to people from all walks of life all around the United States, I've found it interesting that the perception of how something looks, feels, or sounds has a direct connection to people's emotional experience of it. Most of this usually comes from past experience.

I was talking to a guy just the other day who had just gotten a new dog. This dog would run around everywhere and not respond to calls for him to come or stop. Then one day the dog got loose and ran into an area where horses were and, just as the guy was telling the dog to stop, one of the horses kicked the dog. (Don't worry! The dog was not seriously hurt—except for maybe a few bruised ribs.) He did, however, make a connection between that kick and the last word that was said before that kick: "Stop!" After that, whenever the guy said that word, no matter what the dog was doing, the dog would stop, lie on the ground, and stay still until the guy released him.

I choose this particular example here because so many people have been kicked, sometimes pretty badly, by "the church." It is interesting to see how different stimulus, like the look of a church, the music played, or even sometimes the way people are dressed, can have a huge flashback effect.

Past experiences can encompass many different areas and types of interactions within the church. This is not to try to make excuses or endorse more unconventional methods of worship. I'm just saying that some of the "golden calves" of our time might surprise you. Aren't we always looking for tangible things to focus on? We know tangible things are not who or what we worship; we worship the intangible! Still, somehow, churches need to rethink how they try to reach the lost and the hurting. It's okay to make adjustments. We need to remember that the tools we use are not the ones we worship. As the 1960s Peter Scholtes hymn "We Are One in the Spirit" (famously covered in 2005 by the Christian rock band Jars of Clay) goes, "They'll know we are

Christians by our love," not by our song styles, symbols, dogma, or graven imagery.

Decision-making that Grows on Trees

How do you make decisions? Is there a process you go through, or do you just trust your gut and shoot from the hip? Are you more of a design-by-committee kind of leader? Some of the strongest leaders I've ever known or worked with operated by way of some sort of decision tree—a prescribed hierarchical process for looking at a situation and all its parts, and then layering the information gathered over a priority scale that rates specific factors in order of importance.

Having observed this process used by several different kinds of leaders, I recognize how scalable and customizable it is. That is, it can be used to make the smallest decisions, such as what to order for lunch, and also to make enormous ones, such as when it's best to launch a capital campaign and build a new sanctuary.

The process is simple. It's a series of questions that begins with two main ones: "What is the most important thing?" and "What is the highest intent I have for the outcome?" To answer these, you need to know the parts, or subsets, of the decision; the most important things to consider in each part; and the highest intent for each part's outcome. The most important things are those with the most significance, or those that will have the biggest consequence. Figuring out the highest intent is a question of knowing what your true purpose is. Once you figure out these answers, and repeat the process for all its subsets, you've got your parameters—kind of like the box you've built around this decision. (Remember what we learned about parameters and boundaries in Chapter 3: Lead from Outside the Box? Here's where it all starts to connect.) Once you've built the parameters of your decision using the decision tree, you can both find the absolute edges (immovable boundaries) and hone into the more fractal levels and figure things out down to the tiniest detail.

Here's how the decision tree would shake out in our previous example of making a plan for new people who have never been to church before. They're encountering church for the very first time—in *your* worship service. How will you meet their needs? How will you even know what those needs are? We've said the most important thing is knowing your demographic. So that's at the top of the tree. What's the next most important thing? Making sure they feel welcome and comfortable! What is the highest intent? To bring them to Christ and empower them to change their lives for the better by becoming Christians. Now it's time to ask: What are the *parts* of this plan? These are your subset decision questions:

> How will we make sure they know where we are?
> How will we show them what our church looks like?
> Most important? Clarity and accuracy!
> Highest Intent? Make it easy!
>
> What might give them a reason to visit?
> Most important? Tap into an interest!
> Highest Intent? Get them in the door!
>
> What would create an experience that makes them feel comfortable and like they fit in?
> Most important? Meeting them where they are!
> Highest Intent? Bringing them to where God wants them to be!
>
> How will we follow up their visit in a friendly, non-pressuring way?
> Most important? To affirm and connect!
> Highest Intent? Make them want to come back!

You get the picture. When you've drilled down into each subset (and sometimes there can be layers of subsets) with the two clarifying questions—"What is most important thing" and "What is the highest intent?"—you have followed a systematic path for thinking every part of the decision all the way through, anchored to your priority. Best of all, you will have laid a path for others to follow as well.

Put Yourself in "New" Shoes

Now let's play this out in real time with our example of people who've never been to church at all—have no familiarity with it—and arrive at your church.

They walk in, and what do they experience? In more traditional churches, the first thing they may feel when they walk in is lost. (Why are people standing or kneeling? Am I supposed to do that, too? How will I know when to do what?) Because you've put a welcoming team into place and created a simple guide to hand them as they come in, they don't have to wonder.

They may see five books in the back of each row and worry about which book does what, when each book is used, and how to know what page to go to. However, because your intent to make people more comfortable about singing and praying drove the decision to take the books out of the pews and put that information up on screens or in the booklets or cards you handed them when they came in, now these newcomers don't feel lost or confused. They don't have to search for the words, and they're guided through the service, including its songs and prayers. Your intent and the decisions that branched from it made them feel comfortable and part of the group.

When your decisions are driven by shared intent that is rooted in the most important thing (something you've arrived at because you know your demographic) you consistently make decisions aligned with your ultimate priority. The problem is most people don't know why they do what they do. They don't know where the decision or the details of its arrival came from. They haven't really thought about the parts or subsets, or the parts of those parts. I know this seems like a no-brainer, but you'd be surprised how often people fail to ask, "What is the most important thing? What is my highest intent?"

So many churches today do what they do not based on intentional decision-making for their specific demographic. They just want to do what everyone else is doing—especially following those churches that are successful—without stopping to consider their own demographic or their own priorities.

Those Pesky Joneses

It is from an old comic strip created by Arthur R. "Pop" Momand, which ran from 1913 to 1940, that we get the phrase "keeping up with the Joneses" to describe the decisions people make to "keep up" with their neighbors (who they think are doing better than they are at whatever is most important to them). In the original comic strip, it's the social-climbing members of the McGinis family— husband Aloysius, wife Clarice, daughter Julie, and housemaid Belladonna—who are struggling to match the accomplishments and possessions of their wealthier, more accomplished neighbors, the Jones family. When churches adopt the priorities of other churches (the Joneses), rather than drilling down and attending to their own realities, they may find themselves in a mismatch with their demographic. As shepherds, they are at odds with their flock.

Any time I hear a leadership group say, "Well that church is really growing—and here's what they're doing, so we want to do that, too!" I try not to smile as I think of that old comic strip that so totally nailed this aspect of human nature. Then, as gently as possible, I try to guide them onto a decision tree by asking one simple question: Why do you suppose that church is doing that? "I don't know," is usually the answer, followed immediately by, "but it works! Let's do that!"

Not so fast.

Sometimes, when I'm lucky, I know something about the other church, and I am able to tell them the clear intent behind the other church's decisions—and use that as a model for helping them create their *own* decision tree based more on *their* demographic, not based on the church of the Joneses. Usually when I can show them that the other church actually has a very clear intent behind their decision, it's easy to make that shift using this decision-making process as a model rather than just replicating the decision itself.

When the members of a church community know why they're doing what they do (more about that later) and that the choices they make have specific reasoning behind them, they are able to align their decision-making with their priority, such as bringing in new people and helping them feel comfortable. Because they have intent behind what they're doing, they establish the path they're going down together, from top to bottom of the organization. They're not pulled this way or that by the newest, coolest, hippest thing. When they know that they have a plan for their community, and that plan is well communicated, it's easy for everyone to get on board and enjoy the synergy of pulling together toward a common goal.

Will that plan change? Oh, yeah. Everything changes! Leadership isn't a one and done proposition. But with a solid decision tree established, it's much easier to pump the brakes, think about what may need to change and why, run the decision tree down to its smallest subsets, and make a new set of intentional decisions.

With focused intent, a shepherd can lead a flock through times of change, limit the tendency to scatter or be swayed by prevailing winds, and resist being lured by whatever is cool. Leaders with a solid process for making decisions can then fold priority and intent into each decision and all its subsets. If they can communicate this process well and teach others to do the same, their flock stays aligned and the results are driven by this shared intent.

Do You Know What I Mean?

- How do you make decisions? Do you have a prescibed process or decision tree?

- How well do you think your decisions align with the overall intent of your ministries? Is there a measurement you use to test that?

- When have you or have those you lead gotten caught up in what others are doing rather than what is yours to do in ministry? How did that feel? Would you be able to recognize it faster now?

CHAPTER 8
Empower a Hierarchy Flow

Church leaders of today have to have a clear vision honed to a single priority against which every decision is measured.

■

This scenario always starts off great:

"Hey, I have this new ministry idea [insert idea]."

"Wow," the senior pastor says. "That's a really great idea. I'm empowering you to do that, because the result you're describing is fantastic, and I can see you have a passion for this idea. Let's just agree, though, that our number one priority is to love people."

"Right!"

"Okay, great. Go for it!"

But then, down the road and ten decisions later, they're hitting some snags with this new idea, and suddenly everything is off the rails. This may be a scenario you're familiar with in your own ministry. You may be set on making *your* new idea the biggest, baddest thing to ever hit the ministry field, but suddenly things go awry. People are making you angry, because they're not doing things exactly as you want them done. They're always pushing back, getting in your way—and no one seems to get it. (You have the feeling of this is *my* show and I'm going to run it the way it needs to be run and they need to get on board!)

So you push harder and say all the things you think need to be said in the name of getting the job done. Of course, you're sharing these things with others just to make sure *they* understand and see this vision as you see it. Before you know it, you're running over people right and left to make this big idea happen.

Now, what was that number one goal again?

Passion Needs Parameters

The idea of turning people loose with an idea because they have a passion for it is a great thing. But you also have to put some parameters on it. Sometimes you need to say: "Hey, here's the resource bucket you have for that, and if you want more resources, then you've got to go find those resources somewhere else."

If someone has a passion for an idea, a ministry, or a project, and that's what they want to do, that's wonderful! But from a church standpoint, they also have to understand that resources are quite often creative limitations. We only have one building, a set number of rooms (and everybody wants them), and we only have so much money.

I've seen this delegation by passion done well, and I've seen it done terribly. I've seen instances in which an impassioned ministry that someone was empowered to start became as big as the rest of the overall ministry. And, because for whatever reason it was resourced outside of the ministry, it became problematic for the ministry overall. In these cases, I've seen outcomes in which, with the blessing of the original ministry, they parted ways and everyone was happy and fulfilled and the ministry continued to flourish ("Hey, we love what you're doing with this, but you can no longer do it here—go continue that ministry somewhere else as an independent ministry"). I've seen other leaders take a different tactic ("This idea has gotten way out of control and it has become problematic for the original ministry. You need to shut it down"), which, as a leadership response, may have more to do with individual ego than concerns for ministry.

As I see it, if something's flourishing, give it wings. It's really important for leaders to remember their job is always to stay aligned with what *God* wants for a ministry. Going back to the first example, when something gets put on a parishioner's heart to do—and it gets done—then God blesses both parties, the parishioner and the leader, because God thinks it's a good idea, too. When that project or initiative experiences growth, sometimes exponential growth, it might get to the point of you having to say, "Hey, this has gotten big enough, it's been resourced enough, and now it has become a different thing than God wants to get done here. It's on a different trajectory with a different goal." It might require a different decision tree at that point, and the ministries can thoughtfully separate in a healthy, not destructive, way. Making such a change in trajectory does not have be a disciplinary action or a consequence. There's no need to make anyone feel bad when coming to the realization that this ministry is for everybody—not just this congregation—if it's grown too big to stay and needs to go somewhere else. It's still a blessing. It's still what God wants.

So, if for your main ministry the number one goal was unconditional love, and this other ministry, which began as a subset of that goal, has become so big and powerful that it needs to separate, that's all okay. Because its number one goal, while also being unconditional love, may drill down to a very specific *expression* of love that only serves a particular segment of the overall demographic, and this may become limiting to the larger group. Sometimes a ministry that is accomplishing something God wants a person to do doesn't really fit with the mission and ministry the church needs that person to do. Our old thinking and old models make this challenging for everyone.

The critical difference today's leader can make is developing a practice of observing, recognizing, and understanding when this is happening. The key is then being able to release that ministry and that person to go do the job God wants them to do without diminishing its—or the person's—importance or worth.

What if the purpose of your whole ministry, your whole church, was to empower that one person to do this one thing they're doing? What if the impact of that little ministry that has outgrown its banks is the very reason you're where you are, doing what you do?

It's critically important to always support people who are doing what they're called to do. Even if it's not within the goals of your church or your overall ministry, it is your leadership responsibility to learn to stop, step back from ego and power concerns, and just say, "Be blessed and go do that. I'm rooting for you. It seems like a really good thing you're doing."

When you're talking someone through their role in your overall ministry honestly, and you're trying to help them figure things out so they can grow in whatever they're feeling called to do, that's leadership. Helping them form their ideas, find their path, and follow it—that's leadership with a capital L.

A Word About Armchair Quarterbacks

It's easy for people to sit back and complain. It's easy for people to behave like armchair quarterbacks, lounging in the comfort of their living rooms critiquing the athletes and coaches on TV, when they themselves are far removed from the high-pressure experiences felt by those on the field. But when it comes to actually stepping up and having to make the hard decisions, nobody wants to be in those shoes. Because it is hard.

Going back to the hierarchy flow, if a ministry leader can't get behind what the overall ministry is doing, if they can't be a follower of the overall vision for whatever reason, human nature may kick in and that ministry leader may cause destruction by complaining, backbiting, and creating dissention within your staff. It's far better to just recognize when a ministry path is diverging from the main ministry, and it is better for everyone if you just allow that to happen.

Church leaders of today have to have a clear vision honed to a single priority against which every decision is measured. They must also communicate that vision and priority to the entire organization in a hierarchy flow that makes that vision clear and the decision tree understandable to everyone in the organization. Then, when you have passion in your ministries, you have to empower people—and provide carefully thought-out parameters—to follow wherever God is leading them in ministry. When that ministry outgrows its parameters and threatens to topple the priority set for the whole church, it's time for a discerning conversation to decide whether that ministry needs to continue on its path away from the church, or change course to fit back into the fold with the other ministries. All of this can and should be done in love, support, and prayer for what is best and most aligned with what God wants.

This is the kind of thing today's leader has to learn to do differently. We have to teach people this hierarchy and process, and emphasize that all must be done in love and support for what God wants, not what people want. This can be very different from the day-to-day world we currently live in, the world of 24/7 social media, where everyone has an unlimited outlet for expressing their opinions.

By teaching others how you develop and establish your decision trees, you're showing them a new way for making decisions in their own lives, too, independent from the constant deluge of diverging and distracting opinions.

When you start to see people making decisions in this manner, using decision trees as the result of your teaching, you can start trusting them to use this method to make future decisions in whatever ministry level they're in. Even when you don't know the details of their decisions, you know you can trust their method for making them, and that those decisions are aligned with the priority you've established together.

Be a Game Changer

Do even the best leaders make mistakes? Of course they do! We're all human and every single one of us is going to make a mistake from time to time. It's how we *handle* those mistakes that makes the difference.

One of the biggest game changers in this area I've experienced was when I helped start a church years ago with a few friends of mine. It was kind of like a sister church to another bigger church, but also kind of a separate thing.

Everything was going pretty well, and then, as so often happens in churches, there came some tribulation. The "big church" decided to make some significant doctrinal changes that didn't fly too well with the leadership of the affiliated church we started, so we decided to come out from under that other church. The way the leadership of both churches handled things, aligned with the highest priority of love and commitment to following their respective decision trees for a strong hierarchy flow, we were able to part as friends. It was as healthy as it could be.

Before anyone starts to push back on this part, please understand I am *not* talking about church or denominational division. I'm talking about ministries within a church that are growing and thriving and eventually may need to become their own entity. I'm not talking about an I-don't-like-what-you're-doing-so-I'm-going-to-go-start-my-own-church-and-take-all-these-people-with-me situation. That's a very different thing.

Keep Your Check Engine Light On

As leaders, we have to check ourselves constantly against what we say our priority is. Not only do we have to learn to check ourselves (and more specifically, our own egos), we have to teach our team to do the same. That's where leadership comes in. Most people don't know how to do the self-monitoring it takes to keep a ministry on track and aligned with both their vision and the priority established at the top of the decision tree.

Not only do most people not know how to check themselves, but they also don't know how to check one another—in love. As leaders, it is our job to provide the tools our people need to check both themselves and those working alongside them, keeping everyone's hearts and actions aligned with and attuned to the overarching vision without harming their relationships or one another.

Too Many Cooks in the Kitchen

I'm not trying to be militant here, but somebody's got to be the main leader. Somebody has got to have the vision. To be successful, you can't have conflicting visions in the same organization.

The places I see moving forward pretty well, those that are really reaching people and doing great ministry, usually have pretty decent leadership. When I say that, I'm not referring to a single person or group of people, but to the structure under which they lead. In these churches leadership is delegated well, yes, but there is also, to a certain extent, an actual line of authority organized through a clear chain of command.

When I think about that kind of stuff, I always think about the more organic lines of authority, the hierarchy of ministry: God, Jesus, Holy Spirit; then the shepherd (church leader); and then whoever might be below the shepherd. It's a prescribed path for the vision to flow, passing down through the ranks to the people. In the time of kings, there was always a hierarchy of authority that flowed down from the throne.

One thing I see in a lot of other places is "too many cooks in the kitchen," or too many people trying to control, influence, and accomplish something leading to a negative result. When you have people in an organization always second-guessing the leadership, offering their own version of the vision, and trying to maneuver things in that direction, you have conflict. When people are spending their energy in conflict over what the vision is, or should or should not be, you're just wasting valuable time, energy, and brain power.

This is not to say that leadership can't be collaborative. A vision can be created together and individuals in the organization can be empowered and enabled to move forward in their own way to accomplish their own little piece of that vision. If, however, there isn't solid agreement with the hierarchy flow of that vision—who's in charge of what and to what extent—ego-driven power grabs will start to rear their ugly heads. It's just human nature.

This all goes back to the decision tree we talked about in the previous chapter. The leader sets the priority and the parameters, and that's the basis of the decision tree, right? And every single person, every single decision, *every single action*, has to go back to that tree, that priority. If *this* is the most important thing, everything we do has to be subject to that thing. So the parameters of individuals go from wide open to "how does this serve the most important thing."

Focusing only on the most important thing creates a big, wide gate through which everything much pass. Then as we get to the second most important thing, we know that depends on the first important thing, and the gate gets a little smaller. You still have parameters you can work within (remember those boundaries and choices that make the box? Thinking outside the box while staying within the parameters we are given is where that sweet spot of creativity lives). Everything is in service to that big number one goal—the priority set by leadership. The key is to keep checking and rechecking your heart, your actions, and your decisions to make sure that up and down the tree, everything stays aligned with the priority.

That's hierarchy flow.

You Are Not the King

With hierarchy flow, we are looking to God for our mission. It starts with a purpose, then moves to a direction. We've covered some of this already, but what we need to focus on here is who the leader is. To me, the chain of command is simple: God, Jesus, Holy Spirit, and then shepherd (church leader).

As I touched on previously, in times of old we also had a king who had to fit in there somewhere, depending on the king and the era, and now we are pretty used to the words *president*, *general*, and *CEO* as well. They're all totally different, but for this application we will use military terminology.

To begin with, church leaders need to understand that they are not kings. Church leaders have no power other than what is given by the One (God) who called them to do God's work. So at most, a church leader could be a general. As a church leader, are you the only general? No, that's not how it works. You are one of many generals commissioned across the world to lead just one part of the work God has given humankind to do. Can a general be replaced? Most definitely. It happens all the time. However, if your heart is in the right place, it won't matter because you will still be following the king (God) who can call you to a new task at will. So, one of the big things a leader must learn is how to follow. (Kind of a paradox, isn't it?) If you don't know how to follow, then you can never lead well. Great leaders know how to follow.

What are obstacles to following? What do we look for in someone we wish to follow? From my perspective of watching years and years of leadership at all sizes and levels of organization, the people to follow are those who demonstrate the understanding and perception of a plan, knowing what the ideal future holds, and who offer the feeling of making a difference. They are people who themselves feel loved, appreciated, and protected, and who also make others feel loved, appreciated, and protected.

These are the qualities that will drive people to help you in your mission. The sooner you feel these things and figure out how to convey them to others, the sooner you will have people lining up to help you. The problems start when you have a whole bunch of people (and possibly some leaders among them), but no one knows who is supposed to be supporting whom, and it turns into a fight because everyone has different ideas about how to get things done. Going back to our overarching sheep analogy, your herd is committed, but restless and jockeying for position in the pecking order.

What's a Shepherd to Do?

One of the biggest issues I've seen, having worked with hundreds of ministries through the years, is the complete lack of hierarchy. When you make a priority of establishing your heirarchy flow, things tend to settle down and people fall into line pretty well. You're always going to have some strays, some going rogue, some lost lambs, but that's all just part of the package and why you have your crook (that walking stick with the hook on the end of it) to pull them back onto the trail.

Having established a hierarchy, we can move downward from the top. Now I need to be clear here: This is not the kind of hierarchy where you just get to tell people what to do. I'm talking about a responsibility hierarchy. It's a totally different thing. In this kind of hierarchy, you are at the top of the so-called food chain and therefore the most responsible to Christ, the king. This is a place of extreme pressure. You carry the most weight, but you should not carry all the weight alone—that is why you have other leaders to support you, and for you to support.

The Perfect General

If we look at Jesus as the first perfect general, we can see that he had an inner core of twelve people who he laughed with, cried with, rebuked, taught, protected, and most of all loved dearly. He lived life with them and showed them how life is to be lived. He was their best mentor and their best leader. Before he ascended to heaven, he put them in charge as the generals of his new work on earth.

I think it is important to notice that Jesus had twelve disciples. In today's society, we are always researching the best way to do things. One of the best hierarchies we have, one of the best examples of a clear chain of command able to effectively lead large groups of people, mentoring them and building them into an organization that will do what it takes to accomplish a mission, is the military.

This brings me to pyramid hierarchy, which is based on the triangle, one of the most stable shapes in all creation. Let's look at this idea, starting at the pyramid's base. Why did Jesus have twelve people he was directly living life with? Doesn't it seem like there should have been fewer than that? He was God in the flesh, after all! But looking closer, it does seem like the connections that fed down the line kept everyone feeling well-connected, well-loved, and well-mentored, doesn't it? This is the basis of the house church or "home group" church, in which a small group of Christians gather and worship, growing in faith together in a private home. People all feel loved and connected and like they have a say that could be funneled back up to the main leadership in a systematic manner through a methodical procedure, not in a shotgun manner with hit-or-miss effectiveness.

The problem with this type of situation in the current day (because we are *not* Jesus) is that there is usually not a clear picture of responsibility or chain of command. Where do decisions come from? What directions and choices are driving the leadership? Who is going to support the people who are implementing these policies?

Going back to the military as an example of a working hierarchy, we find three parts: volunteer, enlisted, and commissioned officers. Now, keep in mind I am not following the military line precisely; I am just using it as a tool to help us visualize the type of structure, scaled to the size of the organization. Basically, the commissioned pastor or elders in a faith organization are the ones in place to steer the ministry. The enlisted deacons and other heads of departments are the ones who make the ministry happen. Then you have the volunteers who take the ministry to the people; they are the legs of the ministry. This works because there is a clear path of responsibility. When something is asked of people, it is asked from the top down, by leadership, not just by any individual whose personal preferences could take people off in different directions.

I know this may sound controlling, but it is actually very freeing. People can relax when they do not have to make judgment calls, and especially when they know you will support them as they do what is asked.

United Ministry?

Yes, *united ministry* sounds like an oxymoron! Unity rises and falls in leadership, and if you are in unity with your leaders, then it usually flows down the ranks. When done properly, you will have a relationship with everyone on your team who you take care of, plus your team leader who takes care of you.

I see problems with unity all the time in churches when it comes to the music, where the music director is at odds with the pastor about the type of songs that should be included, and the style they should be performed in, and it's always a tension that risks being resolved with a breakup. Instead of leadership coming together and finding common ground and growing together, they are at odds, not living life together, not experiencing the same types of things, and each waking day they grow further apart.

Some of the most destructive words I hear said all the time include "if I had my way" and "they have no idea what people are looking for." These, and other expressions of similar sentiments, are always tearing at the fabric of the church. Imagine the people the worship leader is living life with, the members of the worship team, constantly at battle with one another. Even worse, imagine the sound person, who is only a volunteer, getting heckled from the pulpit when a mistake is made. I feel so sorry for most of these under-trained volunteers who become the scapegoats for badly planned services. These are things I see all the time. And it's very hard not to then laugh when I hear these very same people talking about being united in ministry.

The key to leadership is to have a hierarchy with the right people in place, in an organized fashion, with a clearly communicated plan, and a flow of information and mentoring that is actively taking people to the promised land.

Back to Passion—the Double-edged Sword

As we discussed earlier, having passionate people working with you is a great thing. To try to invoke passion where none exists is more difficult. Sparking passion in your flock requires that you extend a helping hand. You need to help your church members develop a strong belief that they are doing what they are called to do. After goals are set and met, and people get a taste of success and see how their small part of the ministry is changing lives, passion will inevitably grow. It was that type of passion we saw in Exodus 17, when Aaron and Hur came to Moses when he was weak and held his arms up in the air for him until the sun set.

Having an already passionate flock can be easier than having to create that passion. However, on the other side of this double-edged sword (or maybe a two-sided coin if you want to be a little gentler about it), in most settings—and in churches in particular—passion equals drama, and drama is a challenge for many, if not most, ministries. It's just part of our human nature. As one ministry leader pointed out in a casual conversation about why there was always so much drama (and sometimes outright meanness) in churches: When we feel passionate about something (and religion especially qualifies), heightened emotion runs just under the surface of everything. I've seen this and so have you, and it isn't pretty—or productive.

What we are looking for as leaders is the passion without the drama. When a leader knows the heart is in the right place, committed to leadership hierarchy, and aware of and aligned with the master plan, that leader doesn't have a fight at every turn. (Saying that Simon Peter, one of Jesus's twelve apostles, was a "passionate" person is a bit of an understatement.) If these essential elements are not in place, and any perception of weakness is making people feel unprotected, they start feeling the need to protect themselves and their turf, the territory they consider under their control. They feel a need to take control, and then feel distressed about what's next and all the choices that need to be made.

In the Gospel of Mark, the setting for the arrest of Jesus is the Garden of Gethsemane, outside Jerusalem, and it was there, as they were taking Jesus away, that Simon Peter's passion took hold. Oh boy, was there drama! I see it like this: Simon Peter (also known as Peter), feeling overwhelmed with passion, went for it. He got a sword and started yelling and swinging and chopped off the ear of Malchus, the servant of the high priest Caiaphas who was participating in Jesus's arrest. I'm guessing Peter was probably trying to get to one of the priests for leverage.

I love how Jesus redeems this moment, not with scolding or yelling. Not with understanding and healing, either. Jesus knew that Peter's heart was in the right place, and while he loved Peter's passion, Jesus knew that Peter did not yet understand the plan. He used this as a teaching moment for all, telling Peter to put his sword back in its sheath. Jesus understood that the coming events were all part of God's plan.

As leaders, we all need to remember this scene when the drama emerges. We need to know where people are and develop their faith to make them better and stronger when it comes to handling conflict—and drama—in ministry. Guiding, not judging, and building trust and programs that will help the people we lead grow as we grow will make all the difference in keeping things calm and moving forward. Remember, a calm flock, confident in the direction it is moving, on some level knows and understands where it's going and why. The members of the flock feel protected by their shepherd—and are much less likely to stampede or bite one another.

Passionate people are the ones who change things; they are the ones who will say "Yes!" to the challenges of ministry. There is a reason

Jesus put Peter at the head of the class of twelve. Peter was the one Jesus put in charge of building his church in Matthew 16. Passion, when properly channeled, gets good things done for God!

A Word About Conflict Resolution

Like a pendulum swinging freely to and fro, opposing forces are always pushing to one side or the other. "I want this," pushes the pendulum's weight at the bottom to one side. "But I want that," pushes this same weight back to the other side. There are always going to be forces pushing the trajectory, and as leader it is your job to *center* that trajectory.

Conflict in ministry is unavoidable. It's just part of the package. The trouble is, nobody likes conflict—and conflict resolution is hard. Expecting conflict and teaching conflict resolution to others is what helps keep that pendulum centered and still. It's a huge feat—something that today's shepherd must teach as well as model. But too often I see leaders who don't know how to do it. Matthew 18 offers some advice for this (and of course I'm paraphrasing):

1. Go directly to the person who has wronged you and point out the wrong directly (not via text or email!).
2. If the person doesn't listen, take one or two others with you and talk to that person again.
3. If the person still doesn't listen, take it to the church (or I would guess, a pastor).
4. If this still doesn't change the person's heart and mind, you've done all you can and have to let God do the rest in God's own time.

Because human passion and emotions tend to run high in churches, constantly driving the conflict bus, it's sometimes hard to bring those biblical concepts to fruition when tempers are flaring. So, along with all the other roles you have as a modern-day shepherd, being a conflict resolution role model is one of the most important. It's also a role you will fill most often. Invest in training, learn how to check yourself, and then learn how to teach these valuable skills to others to help minimize the time, energy, and relationships lost in conflict that could easily have been avoided or resolved.

Be Willing to Fail

In this day and age, when everyone is worried about this and worried about that, one of the most constricting emotions we can have is fear. Most of the time the fear that consumes and cripples us is not fear of what we should be doing or thinking about. It's fear of the consequences of our bad choices, like eating poorly, driving recklessly, or sleeping around when you are single (or worse, when you're married). But of all the many, many things people typically tend to fear, the biggest fear we face every single day is fear of failure.

More than anything, we fear making the wrong choice. This fear can get us so bound up we don't make a choice at all. All the things we've covered in this chapter (hierarchy flow, passion, managing conflict), which have lasting repercussions in the physical realities of our day-to-day ministry life, depend on us handling the things we feel are in some way scary that we don't want to deal with or make the wrong decision about.

The interesting thing is sometimes it comes down to too many options and, in some cases, peer pressure. Most of us have been conditioned to believe we can do anything we set our mind to, that our self-esteem and self-confidence are what matter most, and that we need to have options in order to be happy. The freedom to make any choice we want may be the best thing that has happened to us, but it also might be what paralyzes us.

Have you ever wondered why so many people are on medication for feeling overwhelmed? Look at the choices we have to make, all day every day! It's a little like being a teenager all over again. For teens, the big world is their oyster, but with so many choices bogging them down, most of the teens I know are scared to death. We all want to be confident that something is possible before we expend the time and effort (and budget) to try to do something we feel called to do.

I remember back when no one other than a professional stunt-person would attempt certain things, like Evel Knievel jumping busses on a motorcycle back in the 1960s. Some stunts, even ones we don't think of as stunts now, were once unheard of. But eventually someone tried something outlandish as part of a one-off spectacle and, over time, people repeated it with more and more frequency. As others launched their own attempts, the measurements of success got bigger and higher and faster and over greater and greater distances.

So often when someone would say, "That can't be done!"

"No way! That can't be done!" everyone would agree. While no one wanted to be the first to try, someone ultimately did. Maybe they failed at first, but once they succeeded, others followed suit.

Fast-forward to today. Some of the newer stunts include doing backflips in the air on a motorcycle while jumping a bus—or three or five busses. At first no one seemed to be able to do these tricks, and yet some would keep trying until they did. There's always a person who's the first to do something previously considered impossible.

I love this famous quote from scientist and businessman Thomas Edison, who said while still testing and inventing the first commercially practical light bulb: "I haven't failed; I've found 10,000 ways that don't work" ("Importance of Thomas Edison's quotes," Thomas Alva Edison Foundation, https://www.thomasedison.org/edison-quotes).

This is the same positive attitude about failure I think the apostle Peter had that made him so perfect for ministry. In ministry you are working with people, and people fail—a lot! The key for leaders is to know this and not care, to be able to see past each failure to the next failure, and past that to the success somewhere in the future. (Despite all the ways that didn't work, Edison eventually did get to success, playing a critical role in modern life with inventions including the incandescent light bulb, the motion picture camera, and improvements to the telephone.)

Another quote from Edison I consider to be a real gem is, "Many of life's failures are people who did not realize how close they were to success when they gave up" ("Importance of Thomas Edison's quotes," Thomas Alva Edison Foundation, https://www.thomasedison.org/edison-quotes). This is where Edison's passion comes into play. (He acquired an astonishing 1,093 patents during his lifetime!)

Passion comes into play for Jesus (the Passion of the Christ) in Matthew 26, when he is in the Garden of Gethsemane crying and praying that this "cup" that is set before him would somehow pass from him. And then we see Jesus's acceptance that God's will, not his own desire, will be done. Modeling this ultimate act of leadership, Jesus moves past it, not discouraged but with a new and fresh determination.

Now, it's important to point out that some ideas are just not good ideas. Another key to good leadership is knowing when to stop, pull the plug, and redirect. We all know that continuing to do things that don't work and expecting a different outcome without changing something in the equation (physically or spiritually) is the definition of insanity.

I've heard the sayings, "Don't get off the horse mid-stream" and "If it worked before, it will work now." To these I say, "Unless the horse is dead. Then I think it's time to get off the horse, mid-stream or not." It's pointless to keep saying, "Giddy up!" when the horse has expired. It makes much more sense to say, "That was a good horse, and I learned a lot, but now it's over and I need find a new ride." And just because something worked once, at a certain time and in a certain situation, does not mean it will work again or can work under any set of circumstances.

Perspective is everything. Learn from the experience of failure; don't count it as a loss. Failure is just information. Take that knowledge and move in a new direction, keeping what you learned and any of the good things—the parts that maybe did work—with you. Leave what failed behind.

On Moving Forward Together

When it comes down to it, it's crucial to know where you are, and what level you're on. Everyone needs to strive to be a little bit better, not for the sake of being as good as others, but to be better than we were and more like Christ. You will never be sinless like Christ on this Earth, so accept that failure as part of the equation; but, because God's grace abounds, like Saul, who became the apostle Paul, we must keep pressing on toward that goal. Christ is our leader, and our goal as Christians is to be like him. It is hard knowing that we are bound to failure in this, but this common ground between all of us can lead us in the direction of grace and kindness (rather than to judgment of others) and toward helping one another to grow where we are lacking. We're *all* on the same path.

This sounds simple, but it can be a difficult thing. As leaders, we are growing in ways that are personal to us, and when we see people struggling with issues we have conquered in our own lives, or issues that are not problems for us, it's easy to get judgmental.

I often hear people saying, "Well, they can't be saved because they use foul language!" (I'm using "foul language" as an example because I know a lot of people have problems with it; feel free to fill in your own example!) The point I want to make is that using bad words is no worse than many other behaviors; however, in certain circles, it is often considered to be socially unacceptable. It's behavior most churchgoers are judgmental about. But regardless of an issue a person may have, I know (and sometimes have to remind myself) that God is working on that part if it is truly at the heart of the person's other problems. If we respond in a negative way to a person who is struggling with some issue we deem inappropriate, we're just turning off an opportunity to lead.

When Jesus spoke to the masses, he didn't say, "Only the people who don't do this, this, and this can come and not be judged." If anything, Jesus did the opposite—he judged the people who claimed, "We are the best and we're doing the judging." I think the lesson to be learned here is found in the age-old questions: What do you think Jesus would have said? Would Jesus have walked away? Or would he have loved them through it? Remember, Jesus went and ate with the worst of the worst—he loved them and did not expect them to clean themselves up before he got there. He was the cleaner.

Going back to our earlier discussion of kings and generals, remember that God is the king. We are just generals (at best!) and probably ranked a lot lower than that. Just because Jesus was able to judge does not give us the right to judge. We are not without sin. Remember that familiar expression from John 8 about how the person who is without sin should be the first to cast a stone against someone who has been found guilty of some other sin?

This calls to mind the time I was at a church service, and I had to get up and leave. Up until this point, I'd had a lot of respect for this pastor—he was a man of good reputation and I had known him pretty well, years earlier. So, I was in this service and could not believe my ears when he actually said, "I am at a point that I am not confined by sin; I don't sin anymore." He went on to say if you are a true Christian, you too are (or will be) free from sin—and if you are not (a Christian? Without sin? I wasn't clear on that.), you are not saved and will go to hell. Well, I just could not sit there and listen anymore, so I got up and quietly left the building. As I left, I prayed for that pastor, and especially his for flock, because I know that only Jesus could change his mind. My judging or slandering him was not the way. That would make me no different.

I did do something though. I removed myself—and that is part of the point. To be a little like Christ is not to try to control others. It's to control yourself. To make sure you respond in a way Christ would. I knew that the only way that pastor could change would be a softening of his heart. Could I have stood up and said, "That's not true!" and made a big fuss? Of course I could have. If I were in charge of that church, I would have probably (gently) tackled him to get him to stop talking, and I would have publicly corrected what he was saying to the people I was directly responsible for. I would have protected my family the best I could.

The takeaway here, for all of this, is all of us are working on things, and we will continue to work on things 'til we die. Even the very best among us are not even close to being sin-free. To say that your sin is less than my sin is a Catch-22—even the smallest lie or moment of self-pride or greed separates you from perfection, and most of the bigger sins are just manifestations of one of the core sins that have been left unchecked to grow like a cancer. As Christians, we continue to battle this spiritual form of cancer every day.

Do You Know What I Mean?

- Have you ever had a ministry overflow its banks and boundaries? Jump the tracks entirely? What did you do? What could you have done differently knowing what you know now?

- What is the biggest challenge you face when leading leaders? When have you been too influenced by others' opinions and how did you get back to the original vision—or did you?

- What is the biggest mistake you've ever made in ministry? How did you handle it? What would you do differently now, assuming you still made the same mistake?

- How do you check and monitor yourself to make sure your decision-making stays aligned with the priority at the top of the decision tree? How do you check and monitor others? Is it done with love? When have you checked or monitored others not through love and what were the consequences?

- When have you felt the fear of making the wrong choice? What did you do? Have you ever allowed yourself to "fail big?" What did you learn?

CHAPTER 9
Guide the Experience

The choices you make about your worship space actively guide the experience of the people you serve.

∎

A shepherd's job is not only to protect and care for the flock, but also to guide—to make good choices that influence and create a positive experience. (You know, plentiful green grass, clean and calm waters, shelter from storms, and safety from predators.) For church leaders, it's really no different. The knowledge, assurance, and lifestyle you're offering those in your care will help sustain them in their day-to-day life, guide them through hard times, and support and protect them from the influence of temptation. The choices you make about your worship space actively guide the experience of the people you serve.

Architecture of Intent
So where does guiding the experience of worship begin? I believe every experience starts with the outside of the building, the architecture of your worship space. Some people feel like a church needs to look like a traditional church, otherwise people won't know that it's the place to come to for help. I think some people feel that a certain type of look and layout is ordained by God to some extent—that all churches should be a white rectangular building with shutters on the windows and a steeple on the top. (Is this because we need a big antenna for our prayers to reach God?)

Please, know my heart here. I'm just trying to have some fun. I believe that this traditional idea of what a church should look like is valid in some communities, based on types of locations and other factors, but these churches will only reach the people they are designed to reach. The look of this kind of traditional building, or at least the public perception of it, can communicate an intent about the *type* of people the church is trying to attract (and convey the message that you are welcome only if you fit this mold). I know that this may sound a little elitist—and it is.

This is what I call *architectural intent*. As people are driving by, we are communicating an unspoken term of qualification. People who are attracted to this type of church may see it as a desirable choice, thinking: "I want my car parked outside so people know I am part of this type of community. This is what I'm about." This is not bad, in and of itself, and I love seeing people connect in such ways. If that is your demographic reach, or your intent is to attract that type of worshipper, then you're on the right track! Keep doing what you are doing, and it will continue to invite that type of person in.

Now let's go to the other side of the spectrum: a church that meets in an old movie theater or a warehouse-style building. This architectural style is the polar opposite of your traditional church-and-steeple architecture. It says, "Blue collars welcome! Relax, and come as you are to this secret 'speakeasy' or clubhouse." What demographic do you think these church leaders are looking for? Is one style better than the other? I don't think so.

In talking to and interviewing people about this, I have found that while there isn't really a wrong answer to church architecture, there *is* a big misunderstanding of it. One space is not more spiritual than the other, no matter what some people may say. The point of all this is if your intent is to reach a specific type of person—or a wider range of people—then you need to make sure your architectural look aligns with your intent.

A case in point: There's been exponential growth of churches constructed with a deliberately nontraditional style of architecture, and these churches have been growing like crazy over the past decade or so. But that, too, is subject to change. Because my company works with churches of all sizes, shapes, denominations, and styles all over the country (I'm always on a plane these days), and since we deal extensively with architectural styles in our AV installations, I'm among the first to see emerging trends in church architecture across the board. Recently, over the past few years, I've started to notice movement back toward more traditional church architecture.

What's interesting is it seems the people who have never been to church are the people gravitating toward the nontraditional styles, and the people who have grown up in churches with more contemporary styles are those looking for something different, and so are now moving toward the more traditional styles. Of course, this is a personal-taste thing and not a hard-and-fast statistic or theological concept, but the trend is noticeable. Still, even with the recent shift toward more traditional architecture, the nontraditional churches are clearly the ones with the fastest-growing church demographic. I believe they will be for some time.

Look Inside

While it's true that sometimes a person can accurately judge a church environment by its architectural design, it doesn't mean a new church member has been successfully secured just because that person may have walked through your church door. Once you've invited people inside with the exterior "look" of the building itself, you have them stepping inside. This is one of the most important parts of the equation. What are your interior spaces telling people? What messages are they quietly communicating? The style and setup of an entry space can say, "Move on through, nothing to see here, go directly to the big room and sit down—and then leave as soon as we're done." Or an entry space can say, "Feel free to get to know the other people in here—and hang out as long as you want to!"

Let's look at a few things that help an entry space say what you want it to say. Key elements to consider are the size of the space, the flow of the floor plan, the functionality of the circulation areas for moving about easily, and the inclusion of a space where people can relax and just be with friends. This can get deep, and go way beyond the scope of this book, but think about what *your* environment is saying. What materials are you using? What colors are you using on the walls? Wall color can have a definite effect on people. This is sometimes hard to nail down because color communication changes over time. A color that says something at one time can say something totally different a decade later.

(For example, the burnt orange shag carpet that was so welcoming in the 1970s became the subject of ridicule, making people cringe and snicker in the 1980s.)

Not only can color date a space, but it affects the emotions of people who enter it, especially for the first time. A room that feels dated may feel uncomfortable to some people but nostalgic to others. Something else to consider is that in different cultures, colors mean different things. While popular or trending colors will shift depending on advertising, marketing, and interior design trends, often these shifts are more shade-based.

If your head is starting to spin, here's a bit of good news: There are a few concepts around color that don't change, that are hardwired into us as designed by God to evoke a gut-level response. Among these are concepts like: Red tends to evoke excitement of some sort—it gets attention, speeds people up, can spark passion, and stimulates a state of alertness; blue usually evokes a feeling of calm and cool, as a color of tranquility, relaxation, and a slower pace; brown typically evokes a feeling of earth, health, and familiarity; and green generally evokes a feeling of growth, new life, and pastoral comforts. The list goes on, and the bottom line is that these are real, gut-level reactions we all share, whether we realize or acknowledge them or not. Most of us are too busy to allow ourselves to get in touch with these emotional responses as we're walking into a room, but that doesn't mean they're not occurring! The way you use this understanding can make or break the interior space you are creating.

All About Tech

How we use technology is an extremely important part of how we communicate. As I travel and consult with church leaders from all over the world, one big question always comes up: "Which element of technology is most important in a church?" Believe me when I say that I love lighting, I love video, and I love architecture, but the answer to this question is easy: Because what we are doing in a church all comes down to sharing the Word of God, sound—audio—is always most important.

When designing a space for sound, the thing foremost on my mind is *distractions*. One of the biggest complaints I hear about worship spaces is that people can't hear clearly. So what do we do? Where do we start? How do we fix or prevent this issue? For me, it all comes back to intent. Here's how I explain the intent of the room being used to communicate the Word of God.

First, I visualize a service in that room, and a new person arriving for worship who has never been in a church before. Where do they sit? In the back row of course, close to the exit.

Now let's walk mentally through the service with that person. The music is nice, the sermon is nice, everything seems to make sense, and the sound is clear.

"But when I think of where I'd put my money," I tell my clients, saving this for last, "At the end of the service, the leader up front asks everyone to bow their heads. This new person, never having been to this type of event, does as instructed. The leader prays and talks about salvation, and this new person can hear the leader as if standing four feet away, even though the leader is a hundred feet away. It feels like the leader is speaking just to them. The room is quiet (no extra noise or distracting echo), the voice is clear and feels close, and as the leader speaks and heads are bowed, with distractions at a minimum, we have cleared the way for the Holy Spirit to have an uncluttered moment in that person's life."

When it comes down to it, that is the priority—why we're here, right? Everything else is icing on the cake. It can be nice to have lights so bright they can burn a hole in your soul—and flash and dance beams all over the room. Video so clear and big you can see the screens from outer space. Bass so loud it will knock the devil out the door! But, as I always tell my clients, "audio and acoustics are where the money needs to go first." All the great architectural features, interior design, rocking music, lights, and video are nothing compared to providing this one, undistracted connection between a person and the Word of God.

You can have the best-designed service in the most beautiful building in the world, but if it sounds like a tunnel to that visitor in the back of the room, or if people in the seats feel miles away from the leader who is speaking, then you are missing the boat. You will never get that undistracted connection that transforms lives.

Many studies have been done on the distraction and anxiety caused by noise pollution in over-reverberant spaces (known in my business as "bad sound"). It has even been proven to cause or worsen negative physical reactions. Think about how much time and energy your brain requires to decipher what someone is saying when there is competing noise. Think about trying to have an important conversation in a crowded restaurant. It's frustrating and exhausting, no matter how much you want to hear and understand what is being said!

Imagine people trying to listen to a message that could change their lives, but what they hear is mumbling or an annoying echo, or sound that is so mashed together they find themselves struggling to focus on the message. Their minds wander, and it's suddenly like listening to Charlie Brown's teacher (or any of the adults who speak in Charles M. Schulz's *Peanuts*). Imagine trying to listen to a message when you can't localize where the sound is coming from, forcing your ears and your eyes to work separately as your brain overprocesses it, trying to make it feel better and as if you are hearing what you see from the correct direction.

Bad sound influences people who are innocently sitting in your space trying very hard to listen to what you have to say. You never know when life-changing moments will happen for someone in a church, but that's why they came, that's why you're there too. Time after time in my work I find this is a simple thing most leaders get wrong. They don't understand that one of the most important parts of their role is to effectively communicate the Word of God to their congregation. It's so ironic that most people think of this last when the bottom line is: If people can't hear the Word of God effectively, why are we doing any of this?

Making It Personal

The key to creating a positive sound experience in your worship space (that clear, clean, moderated, and evenly distributed sensory perception that the leader is standing four feet away from each and every person in the room) is making the room acoustics and the sound system work together to reproduce the human voice clearly and without distraction for every seat in the room. This sounds much simpler than it is and, if you have accomplished this feat, you are doing better than 90 percent of the churches in America I know of! This is a science misunderstood by many, if not most, church leaders, and I'm here to bring the understanding that will help put you in the top 10 percent.

Once you have that basic sound design in place, you can move on to making it louder for a full band. Please don't go out and get the big, loud system and spend all your money on amazing speakers without fixing the room the speakers will be in. Without addressing the architectural acoustics, even the best equipment will sound bad because the room sounds bad. It's a big, heartbreaking waste of money that drives me crazy, and I see it all the time. Many people overspend on things that actually make their sound issues worse! Then they come to us to fix it, but they have no budget left. You would be much better off fixing the room and buying a cheaper system—the end product will still sound much better!

It is beyond the scope of this book to go too deeply into how you fix problem spaces or the physics of the universe. (That could be a whole other book: *You Don't Know Sound.* Yes, I'm kidding. About the other book, that is. But I digress.) What you need to know is we all have innate physical reactions to audio. Once you understand that, and know what triggers positive and negative responses, you can use this knowledge to your advantage. Certain sound qualities can make you feel happy, sad, annoyed, and even depressed. Sound is a powerful thing, and it's one of the most important connection points to the people you are leading.

This begs the question: Why do church leaders leave this important task to someone who has no concept of how these things work and no professional ear for what "good audio" sounds like? I see this all the time. People with no clue how to run a sound system or how the whole thing is put together are running the most important connection point to the people they are there to lead.

To correct this, once the sound qualities of a worship space have been assessed and addressed, the next thing to look at is staffing. You may have people running your sound who are good people trying hard to do a good job, but the needs of this position really come down to talent and experience. You would never ask someone to teach you something if that person has only read the manual and has a surface-level understanding at best, would you? Sound personnel are so often overlooked and undervalued in ministry, when they are literally the ones who can make or break your connection to the people.

When church leaders start to realize this and make the necessary staffing additions, sound quality in worship will improve in countless worship spaces across the nation and around the world! Some of the bigger ministries I work with that understand the importance of sound engineering in guiding the overall worship experience make sure they have the best sound engineer they can afford in this position. Even smaller churches are starting to get it! In fact, I just learned that one of the smaller churches I work with just added an audio professional as their first paid non-pastoral staff position! Once church leaders understand the importance of sound quality and prioritize achieving it, it shows in how they connect with their congregation.

The Art and Science of Lighting

Lighting can also have a huge impact on how people feel in your worship space. The understanding of lighting dips back into color science a little bit, but that doesn't mean we are putting up purple and green lights to make your service look like a disco. (I think I just dated myself.) When we talk about color in lighting, we're talking about the color within what we call "white light."

Think of the type of light that was in your principal's office at school. That dreaded almost-blue tint that enveloped both the space and everyone in it, making things feel cold and not very comfortable. (I got in trouble a lot, so I know this light all too well.) Now think of the light from the fire at a campout with family or friends that made you feel warm and cozy. Even though the heat from the campfire caused some of this feeling of warmth, it is actually the *color* of the light we react to most. That campfire color of light is more like the incandescent light bulbs most of us grew up with in our homes. Because these are now being replaced by newer LED lighting systems in homes, offices, and schools, everyone has to learn the difference between "warm" (yellow) and "cool" (blue) light!

Now that you understand the basics of the different styles of light (and of course there are many nuances, but this is a good start), you can begin to get a picture of how light can influence how people feel in your worship space. If you want to make someone feel warm and comfortable, what type of light would you use? What if you wanted people to move out of one area and into a different area, how would you use light to do that? Can you really influence people's behavior through lighting? I see many churches underuse lighting. I think the power of lighting isn't understood as the leadership tool it can be!

Focus: Leading with Light

Let's consider an event. Everyone comes into the room and the houselights (the lights above where people are sitting) are up and bright, and the stage area is dark. Why is this? It's because we want the people who come into the space to focus on each other. We want our lighting to encourage them to talk with one another, mill about, find the people they know, introduce others, and make connections.

What about when we want them to stop that initial visiting period and sit down and pay attention to what's on stage? We have two options for guiding people to their seats. The first is we can get up in front of the stage and tap on the microphone so it feeds back or makes some sort of noise that gets attention, and say, "Will everyone please take your seat?"

Or we can lead them with light.

As the houselights dim, the stage lights gradually get brighter, and suddenly, like magic, people stop what they are doing, sit down, and look at the stage. Is it magic? No! It's lighting design! You see, God designed *us* to look at and pay attention to the brightest thing in the room (and also to look at God as the brightest thing in the universe, but that, too, is covered more fully in another book you are probably already familiar with). Because our attention naturally goes toward the light, lighting is a very useful tool to guide people, and to guide a person's experience. It is scientifically proven that you can control the attention of an audience based on the contrast of light and dark in a room. Moreover, you can use this awareness, and intentionally use specific lighting, to help people focus on what you want them to pay attention to.

During the many years I worked at Sight & Sound Theatres in Pennsylvania, which was, at the time, the largest Bible-based theater in the world, one of my favorite things was handling set changes with the curtain open. How this works is we would have a small set downstage, at the front of the stage near the audience, that we would light very brightly. The rest of the stage was dark, but you could see enough to set up the next scene, so we would be in the darkened part of the stage working to set things up and change the whole look of the stage. When we did this, I would be looking at the people in the audience as I was standing there, mid-stage. I could see them just fine and, if they had wanted to, they could have seen me, too, but they didn't notice me at all. They were fixated on the brightest part of the stage, hyper-focused on what we had guided them to focus on.

When we were done with the transition, I would always run offstage and go to a door beside the audience (this was the best part for me), and when the lights would suddenly go up on the rest of the stage, the audience would gasp! I would listen to their comments, things like, "How did they do that?" or "They must have a huge elevator!" All of these questions and theories were going through the minds of the people, and I would just smile and think to myself, "The audience was looking at me the whole time and still they did not see!" I even tested this from time to time from a seat in the audience, and even though I knew the trick, I also found myself hyper-focused on the brightly lit area and was oblivious to the workers resetting the scene. What a powerful tool.

I'm not saying that this is the way to do your services, but now you can see why people in many faith venues are making their house darker. Still, this decision shouldn't be made because it's the cool thing to do. It should be about intent. It frustrates me sometimes, when churches are solely focused on keeping up with the Joneses (let's do our lighting just like so-and-so does it—they are growing so fast and, if we do what they're doing, we will, too!) But either way, once you understand at least the basics of lighting design, you'll be able to use these principles to your advantage.

As with just about everything else in the world, you have to find the best compromise for your space and your culture. I often work with leaders who want to move in this direction, but they are met with a lot of resistance, especially from the older generation, and rightfully so. Many older church members view production elements like lighting design as a fad, and if you don't understand (and can't explain) the reasons for overhauling all the lighting in your worship space, it will be hard to get them on board. (You have to put yourself in the place of those who've seen skinny jeans come and go at least three times in their lifespan, and still don't understand the attraction.) But what I've found is, as soon as you help them understand the intent, and how and why lighting design works to produce a result everyone wants, even older members tend to get on board and even get excited.

Speaking of taking care of your older people, I've been working with my dad who is getting up there in years, and he is having some problems with falling and things of that nature. Recently, as I started seeing things more through his eyes, I realized that most older people are worried about two things: how to get up and move from one place to another, and how to not fall while doing that.

I heard about a study of functional alcoholics (who can do things in a normal-looking way despite habitually being under the influence of and misusing alcohol) and alcoholics who can't seem to hold their liquor and are more obviously under the influence, tripping and stumbling and looking drunk. Even when the blood alcohol levels were the same, people observing this second group would describe them as "more drunk" than those in the "functional" group. The study goes on to say that the reason for this difference is that functional alcoholics have a plan. In testing, their reaction times are about the same, and judgments when encountering new obstacles are at the same level, too. Functional alcoholics plan ahead to balance their slower reaction times; they have become accustomed to making plans to get them to and from where they need to be, and they have learned to use their muscle memory differently from people who are not used to living with a fairly constant impairment.

What does this mean to us? And what in the world does it have to do with lighting design and elderly church members? It's not that our older church members are functional alcoholics. It's about how they operate. Many in our elderly population have some kind of impairment—poor eyesight, partial hearing loss, slower reaction times, general fragility, muscle weakness, etc.—so they think differently about changes to their worship space. They have developed plans to navigate their spaces, and they need assurance that they are going to be safe and cared for. So how do we take care of their needs and also reach the goals of our intended focus control?

This is where the compromise comes in. We need to make sure that if we're making changes to the lighting, the lighting design includes clear paths of light to illuminate the walkways. The light can be made a little brighter near exits and in the back of the space to make it easier to see the way out, and extra light can be focused on the exits to help people who need a plan feel more comfortable, knowing that their plan will still be easily attainable.

Contrast Commands Attention

Now let's talk a little about contrast. Contrast is the difference between the brightest and the darkest things you can see. People can experience the same ratio of contrast in different ways and, as our eyes adjust over time, the contrast ratio changes so what might seem dark when you walk into a room from outside seems just right within thirty minutes. The key concept for using contrast wisely is finding the level most comfortable for your demographic.

People respond to lighting levels differently, and those levels subconsciously communicate your intent. For example, to give a feeling of openness and spaciousness you'd want higher brightness, with everything—walls, floor, and ceiling—being evenly lit. For a more public gathering feel, you would still want bright, even lighting, but only from the top down, casting only in the areas people are walking. To provide a more relaxed feel, you'd want lighting that is at a lower level of intensity and a little less uniform, a little spottier, with more contrast between brighter and darker areas. Going back to our earlier discussions of intent, this is a place to put some serious thought into what message you are trying to send to your people—and how you'll keep that message consistent.

Now we move to the stage, chancel, or whatever focal points you have in your worship or meeting space. If you want people to look at something, you need to have contrast. With the brighter, more open "spacious look," it is very hard to create a focal point since everything in the space is lit brightly and evenly. So, what happens to the attention of the people in a space like that? They can look wherever they want to. Even if you have all the seating facing forward, without lighting contrast in that space, you have given them the freedom to look at *everything.* In these spaces, distractions abound, whether it's the kid picking his nose over to the left or the pretty girl who just walked in and sat over to the right. When things have no focus, we may even look at the walls for dirt! Without lighting contrast, the only thing that might attract attention is movement, but even then, it would take a pretty constant amount of movement to keep your attention focused.

Allow me to introduce lighting contrast. The more contrast we provide in our lighting design, the more *focus* we create. This means that, by percentage, the brighter light should be on the stage, platform, pulpit, or on whatever area you desire focus. The darker we have all the other parts of the room, the greater the focus will be on that designated area of focus. Remember how when I worked at Sight & Sound we changed an entire stage set within plain sight and no one noticed? It's the same powerful principle here.

One thing to note as a compromise is that you can design a room to be pretty bright in the center of the space with controlled lighting that only points down, and still create the feel of a darker room, keeping the light off the walls and stage so it is focused only on one area within the space. That way you can create the look of contrast you'd have in a darker room, but still have plenty of light to read by. The key in this scenario is keeping the bright light on the focal point, the brightest thing in the room, and off the walls. Then, when you want to re-create that spacious feel, all you have to do is turn the wall lights back up.

Color Shades Perception

With just one color of light we can do a lot, but to create truly nuanced lighting that influences behavior and perception, use additional colors. Imagine this: You have the room set up so you can change the color of the walls on stage and all around the seating area. Now imagine you're going to be teaching about hell. So you start with a light and fluffy intro, and all the colors in the space are blue and relaxing. Then suddenly you say, "Today we are going to talk about hell!" And just like that, all the walls go from nice, cool blue to bright red! Get the picture? I'm not saying this is what you want to do—or that it's a very good idea—I'm just making a point about the impact that strategic, intentional use of color in your lighting design could offer. (People would sure remember that time you talked about hell!) So that's how color can be used in lighting to transition people and to evoke a mood.

Let's talk about how this might work in the real context of worship. We start the music and the first song starts out slow, so maybe we begin with a soft-blue light scape. Then the song picks up a little in tempo, it gets a little peppier, and we start to move into an orange sunrise-like light. As the energy of the song gets a little higher, we might take it to a yellow, then a red. We keep it in those hotter, more exciting shades, and then maybe the song goes into talking about Christ the King, and we transition into purple.

None of these are hard-and-fast rules, and there's a lot of room to play with dramatic or more subtle shading that can coordinate with the music. Intentional lighting design has a lot to do with visual art, but it's also important to have a basic understanding of how color affects emotion. By design, people's perceptions of what they're hearing can be guided using colored light, arguably much more effectively than just having someone standing and singing. It's a big opportunity to enhance parishioners' emotional connection with the music in a way that sticks with them and melds with the other messaging in the worship service.

Video Transports Imagination

Remember that old saying that a picture is worth a thousand words? Multiply that by twenty-four pictures per second, and you can see the impact of a video. Video is yet another tool now used more and more in modern faith culture. While video is relatively new in terms of ever-evolving technology and the newer and newer things we are able to do with it, its roots are as old as time, going back to the simple drawings people once did to illustrate a concept or tell a story. When looking at the old paintings and stained-glass work in the great cathedrals and other worship spaces around the world, the power of a picture is evident. I'm not going to get into whether the mental picture someone developed to create those works of art are biblically accurate accounts. Regardless, they are great examples of how images help us visualize more abstract concepts.

Jesus didn't use video. (As he was God in human form, he really didn't need video to make his point.) However, there is a vivid use of special effects in Matthew 21 when Jesus tells a fig tree, "May no fruit ever come from you again!" and it withers at once. Because I'm not Jesus, I can't wither things at will. However, if I wanted to make that point, I could use a little video tool and, BAM! I could show you a tree withering right before your eyes, on a screen. Jesus did a lot of visual things to show people a powerful connection to the truth he was speaking about. He also told a lot of stories that encouraged people to use their mind's eye to develop a visual timeline. In those days, people had to cultivate a well-developed imagination—unlike the people of today who are visually spoon-fed.

We've already talked about how the brightest thing in the room is what everyone looks at. Taking this to the next level, it's the brightest thing *that moves* that actually grabs the most attention. For video to be seen, it has to be the brightest thing in the room. Quick lesson: When thinking of a screen, think of that screen at the *black level*, meaning no matter what color the screen is, whatever is projected onto it needs to be so bright it makes the screen seem black in contrast. If you have a screen that is in bright light before you project anything onto it, you will need an even brighter projector to overcome the light that is already hitting the screen. In this case, your projector should be able to project many times brighter light than whatever light is hitting the screen. This is why a movie theater is so dark—so that they don't have to have a brighter projector. It is also why when your projection looks washed out, turning down the room lights makes the image look better.

Awareness of this concept of motion is important because it can either be used intentionally as a great tool of focus, or be very distracting if we don't know how to control it. People will look at whatever is moving, so if you're trying to connect with people, you need to make sure nothing moves except the person or image you want them to look at.

In worship we have a lot of movement because we take people on a journey. Worship should not be about having people locked into just looking at the leader, but more about bringing people together and telling a story. Most of this story is in the words of the music we sing together, and that is great because we can post the words on the screens as they are being sung to reinforce the message visually and help people to learn.

There is a second step, too: You can use imagery to transport people. I was teaching a class on a tour I did a few years ago, and a pastor came up at the end of the class and said, "I hear what you're saying, but I just don't get it." As we talked a little bit more, I could tell he needed to see it to understand. It just so happened that I had heard the band practicing a song they were going to do, and I knew what was going to happen with the visuals. I took him into the place where the concert was starting.

Here's the setup: We're in a big room with very nice sound and equipment and a huge screen behind most of the fifty-foot-wide stage. All you can see from the audience is the band in front of a sixty-five-foot-wide screen that takes up most of your view. It feels like an Imax theater in there. The band starts and the song is soft, with acoustic guitar and my friend Brian Doerksen singing about the universe and how God created it from nothing. As he sings the words, Steve, the video jockey (VJ), is running a video from a satellite scanning the Milky Way. This image fills the screen, and it is awe-inspiring.

As the song progresses, Brian sings about how Jesus is the lion of Judah, and in that instant, the universe image dissolves into one of a lion running across grassy hills. It's an animated lion (a really cool-looking one, not cheesy) that is *gain running* (bounding as if running up a hill), almost frolicking, and the song's intensity builds just a little. At this point it is still a pretty soft song, and then Brian sings, "with a lion's roar," and as soon as he says "roar," the electric guitar comes in with this awesome growl and the rest of the band hits their chord all at the same time, taking the volume from softer to rocking. At the same time, the video is still rolling, and the lion on the screen rears back and *roars*, so now there is an overwhelming crescendo that has all the senses working together at the same time—it still gives me goosebumps thinking about it! Every hand in that place went to the sky in praise. It was an experience. It was art. It was *intention* at work.

When I looked over to the pastor I had been talking to about how all this works, he had tears streaming down his face. He looked back at me and said, "I get it." In that moment he fully understood what I was talking about. Now I know what you're thinking. "Yes, David, that sounds amazing for a concert, and I'm sure you had the top band and the top video screens and the top-of-the-line everything in that space, and that is why it worked so well." Or you might be thinking, "Yeah, I bet it was quite something, but that's way too showy for my congregation."

That is not the point I'm trying to make. You don't need to do things exactly like we did, or do any of these things, for that matter. What I need you to understand is that the intent behind what we did was to create something that affected people in that moment. We wanted to take people on a journey, however emotional, to tell the story in a deeper way. We wanted to make a lasting impression, and video was part of that vision.

I am not into the emotional manipulation of people to get them to feel more attached or to give them some false "experience" that makes them feel closer to God. (That's the Holy Spirit's job.) I'm here to remove the distractions and lead people to a place that I feel led, and if they meet God there, that's great. My job is to set the mood.

I do have a pet peeve when it comes to video. It's the overuse of image magnification (or "Imag" for short). Don't get me wrong, it can be a very useful tool, but if you are less than sixty feet away from someone and can easily see them, you don't need to have a video of them too. It's distracting! Remember, people always look at the brightest thing that moves, and that video image is going to be the brightest thing, so even if they can see the person who is speaking just fine, people will almost always look at the projected image instead, if it's in a comfortable range.

Projecting Imag video of a speaker in a worship space has a few pitfalls to consider. For one, it disconnects people from the person speaking. Have you ever tried to talk to someone who was looking in a different direction? It's not fun, and you can't really connect with them because it feels like they are not paying attention.

In a smaller space, if the screen is near or behind the person speaking, the people will look at the screen instead of the speaker. Now, in a larger space you can locate the screens in places where they aren't in view of the people in the front, so the people toward the front can create that more intimate connection with the actual speaker, and the people seated farther away in the back rows are given the ability to see the speaker's facial expressions and gestures. Because the screen offers a zoomed image of the speaker, it connects the speaker with those who can't see well from where they're seated. There's a lot more to screen placement, Imag applications, and other considerations that are beyond the scope of this book, but these are the basics. Just be sure to go back to intent and the overall feel you're trying to create before you consider using your screens for Imag.

Before we leave this topic, one more word about distractions and focus when it comes to the use of video: When someone comes up to the front to speak, all other movement needs to stop. This means no moving lights, no moving images, nothing moving except the person speaking. Even the tiniest movement will distract most people. Think about it this way: Have you ever watched a movie with the subtitles on? Even if you can hear just fine, your eyes always move to the bottom of the screen every time something pops up, right? This is the same principle at work. We are all hardwired to be attracted to motion. Don't fight it, just understand it, and use it to guide people's attention to where you want it to go.

Do You Know What I Mean?

- Have you ever seen people in a room being guided by its lighting? Have you ever purposefully used this understanding of how attention works in your worship services?

- Have you ever been in a situation where the sound system was somehow distracting? What do you remember more—what was said during the program, or the screech or echo and difficulty concentrating? When has a powerful moment in worship had something to do with sound? How could *you* use sound differently?

- Have you ever considered motion as a tool of focus? When it comes to managing attention and focus in your worship space, what could you do differently to help people focus and absorb more of your message?

CHAPTER 10
Tap into the Power of Music

Music is one of the most powerful tools we have in our entire leadership arsenal for connecting and inspiring people.

∎

This may seem like a funny place to put a chapter on music. We've been in the weeds of worship minutiae. We've been digging around in brain science and how it intersects with leading passionate groups of people. Shouldn't the music chapter be more with the worship stuff? Not so fast. We've been talking about brain science and behavioral neurology, and nowhere is this reality more prominent than in how people connect, respond, internalize, and project emotion in the realm of music. Let me explain. Music is a gift that God has given us. It can do things that cannot be replicated with drugs or with just about any other influence. It is life-changing and can bridge gaps across cultural and language barriers.

Many studies have assessed and continue to assess the neurological connections we have with music. From qualitative research on the impact of music-based interventions for people with dementia to the restorative effect of tapping into musical memory, it's been established that music is so much more than just something fun to listen to. There are numerous accounts of people who do not respond to medications, physical touch, or just about anything else, who—despite this seemingly catatonic state—begin tapping their feet and hands and bobbing their heads when a certain type of music is played.

I witnessed this personally when watching some youth choir kids singing in a nursing home, and a man who had not spoken, or even acknowledged that they were there, suddenly began singing. His face lit up, and he was alert and very much present with these young people. The transformation was incredible. When the music stopped and their program was over, he was able to speak with the kids who stopped by his chair, one by one, to say hello and engage him in some conversation. I watched as he told them about his favorite things, and from time to time he joyfully broke into songs that touched him when he was young, as he remembered earlier parts of his life.

It doesn't take much to find instance after instance of music bringing people who were somehow compromised back to themselves in this way. "Musical perception, musical emotion, and musical memory can survive long after other forms of memory and cognitive function have disappeared," writes Dr. Ronald Devere in his 2017 *Practical Neurology* article, "Music and Dementia: An Overview." According to Dr. Devere, music "can improve mood, behavior, and in some cases cognitive function, which can persist for hours and days after the music stops. Music also does not need to be familiar to exert these improvements and one does not need to have any formal knowledge of music or be musically inclined to enjoy music and respond to it at the deepest level" (Robert Devere, MD, "Music and Dementia: An Overview," *Practical Neurology*. June 2017. https://practicalneurology. com/articles/2017-june/music-and-dementia-an-overview). Music has the unique power to reaffirm personal identity and social connectedness.

Music also has the power to help us learn. Growing up, whenever it was hard for me to remember things, my mom taught me to put a melody to it. This worked really well, and some of my fondest memories of early learning were from songs like "Conjunction Junction [what's your function]," from the 1970s show *Schoolhouse Rock,* which still makes me smile. Even the alphabet, when set to that familiar melody (you know the one), became so much easier to get my head around and remember. As we grow in knowledge, we tend to make everything more complicated, but there is still power in simple songs like the nineteenth-century hymn "Jesus Loves Me [this I know]." You may think to yourself, "What a simple song," but that song has had a huge impact on me since childhood.

When I think of the power of music, I can't help but remember the Old Testament story of how King Saul's anxiety and depression could only be soothed by David playing music for him. King Saul understood (even without all the neurological studies we have access to today) what a powerful tool for comfort and leadership music could be.

A smattering of scientific findings in the field of neurology are now telling us that not only is music a useful intervention for older adults as a tool for enhancing and connecting memories, but also that the brain networks making these links are different from those involved in other types of memory.

Music Is a Connector

Studies have shown again and again that the connection of people who do music-related things together as part of a group, things like clapping in unison, marching, and singing, feel more connected to one another and are more likely to do things for one another, even when they have no relationship with each other outside of this experience.

What does this have to do with leading people? How are we to use this enormous and complex tool God created called music? As leaders, we have set goals. We have identified the place where we are going. Now is the time to bring the people together, point them toward the One we look to for everything, and tell them the deep truths that will resonate. This brings us to why this chapter belongs here. The primal power of music has been proven again and again, and we are looking to rally the people for the work, God's work, we have ahead of us. Because music is one of the most valuable tools in our entire faith-based leadership arsenal, learning to use music effectively is key to connecting and inspiring people.

Because musical options are seemingly limitless, you have choices to make. Music comes from all over the globe and spans thousands of years. Will you use traditional music? If so, from where and when? Will you incorporate the musical scales and tonal structures found in the traditional songs and melodies of East Asia? Or those found in the traditional music of Latin America or elsewhere? What about musical accompaniment? Will you play melodies on the same instruments used by composers in Europe in the 1700s and 1800s?

Maybe you set traditional sounds aside and try to connect with today's culture by using songs from the 1960s and 1970s "Jesus people" movement. No? But Keith Green and Larry Norman really got what Jesus wanted us to know! (I hope you know sarcasm when you read it.)

Faith leaders today have a responsibility to study, know, and balance the relevant sounds and movements of current culture, the truth of scripture, and what they are most comfortable with. Pretty much everybody tends to think (unless they've had a bad experience) that the way they first heard church music—whatever the style may be—is the best way for church music to be. Their preferred way is the way it got stuck in their own heads. However, leaders also have to remember it's not just their own headspace that needs to be considered.

The same style that comforts one person can be a stumbling block for another. There are people who have a visceral response to hearing a hymn being played on an organ because it takes them back to a time or place when they were not shown grace in a faith environment. Some people who once suffered at the hands of organized religion may have only returned to church because there are now other ways to experience meaningful worship. Still, there are others who just don't like modern faith music. The Christian rock genre gives them a headache and turns them off.

Different cultures resonate with different styles of music, too. One of the funniest movies I've ever seen illustrate this is the 1979 comedy *The Jerk*, in which actor Steve Martin plays the role of Navin Johnson, a white kid who grew up in a Black family who adopted him as a baby. In the beginning scenes, Navin would try his hardest to sing along and clap and stomp to the beat in his family's sing-alongs, but he could never get it. He tried and he tried and still never got it. One night, he had the radio on and it switched programming. The music that came on was a different style of music and, all of a sudden, he could tap to it, clap to it, and he was instantly connected. In this scene he dances around the house, waking everyone up, saying, "This music speaks to me!" Even though this is an intentionally silly scene, it illustrates the different connections people make with music. A classic trap church leaders fall into is trying to fit all people into one style of worship.

There is no right or wrong style and one is not more blessed than the other. Many of the old hymns were on the Top 40 lists of the best-selling audio recordings in their day. Music is not about popularity; it's about offering a vehicle to carry God's truth into people's lives. The musical style you choose for this vehicle is a demographic question, not a spiritual one. Because God's truth is the Truth, the style of its vehicle is not important.

Know your people. If you're in New York City with a young, urban congregation, country music is probably not the style to go with. I've worked with people who will by default play the old hymns, saying, "That's what everyone remembers and it's the music the church was built on." I just smile and say, "Oh yes! I remember that time Jesus and the disciples broke out into that song." (More sarcasm.)

Please hear my heart. I love some of those old hymns. I feel their greatness in my bones. When I hear them, it takes me back to when I was young. But the people who don't have this context or connection to the old hymns—or even to modern religious songs—don't relate, so forcing *your* connection on them is probably not the best way to reach them. Think about this: In the Old Testament God even changed the dietary laws of the people so they could move into a different culture. He did not alienate them due to their differences and personal tastes.

Because music is such a powerful medium, it is also a powerful teaching tool for leaders. It is well-documented in the scientific community that the truth you speak will only last a few minutes in the minds of people listening to you, and only if you repeat your points over and over will they be able to store them in their longer-term memory.

If you plan your worship well, you will select songs that wrap around the truth in your message. These music selections will help build upon every thread of this truth, and the people will repeat that truth in song, refrain after refrain. (Maybe they'll even like it so much they'll listen to it in the car, too, reminding them of the message you shared.) So, the connection points we have with music are many. And best of all, the connection or bond with a song and its underlying truth can become a long-term, long-lasting connection with your message.

Am I saying that if we just choose songs to fit our message, we'll all sing them and everyone will get it? If only it were that easy. To fully understand this concept and what a powerful tool music can be for your leadership, we'll need to go a little further and take a shallow dive into song structure (I know, you did not sign up for music theory, but bear with me—it's going to be worth it).

The Structure of Music

We all know that different types of music can set different types of moods, and playing music at different levels can change the feeling and sensation we get from it. We live in a very compressed society where information is pushed into smaller and smaller spaces to save time or space. This compression has its pros and cons. Here's an example you're probably very familiar with. Take a well-written email and compress it to a text message formed out of acronyms, initialisms (acronyms pronounced as individual letters), and abbreviations. Sure, your brain can unscramble the meaning, but you may not be getting the full picture of the communication the way you would have from that full, well-written email. That is what a lot of modern music has been turned into, compressed into its simplest form, and this compression takes a lot out of the original meaning.

     I was at a church the other day in Massachusetts in the Boston area, and I noticed the CD player had been removed from the AV system. When I asked the pastor why he removed the CD player, his answer was great: "People stopped bothering to learn a song to play it live," he said. "They just started playing a CD and singing along to it instead." He continued, saying that he noticed the youth were becoming disinterested in learning to play instruments, and would instead opt to play the CD. This led to their not involving others. They couldn't be bothered to take the time to communicate the vision for a song and how it connected with the message. In some cases he noticed that, due in part to the social media world we're now living in, they had lost the ability to communicate effectively with one another in general. So he took the CD player out.

     "We are only going to have live music," he told them, "And we are going to do it well." He wanted a high standard of music, and when I found myself in a room with those kids, they were fantastic—and they were young! (Someone there told me I ought to stick around and hear the youth band—they were even better and only a little bit older!)

A couple of things struck me about this conversation and the observations that followed. First, was how the people responded to this pastor's removal of their CD player and the shortcut it offered. From all reports and appearances, they didn't really mind once the decision was made that they would only do live music. Second was how this decision resulted in the involvement of more people and forced them to learn to communicate better.

The experience built an even bigger core of leaders, bonded by their music and the benefits of learning the proper way to communicate with each other around the creation of live music. What a great opportunity that church leader created to guide these reluctant musicians in the interpersonal relationship-building needed for a strong leadership team! It is easier to guide people when they are focused on learning a new skill together. Everything works better when you empower a large group of people to learn to communicate, with give and take, to achieve a common purpose and goal.

Synchronous Side Effects

This brings me to the next thing I see relevant to the nature of leadership—the physical nature of how moving together creates a stronger bond. In her 2020 *Scientific American* article, "Moving in Sync Creates Surprising Social Bonds," science journalist Marta Zaraska reports on the powerful effects of this phenomenon. "Many group activities boost our sense of belonging," Zaraska writes, "but research shows that doing things synchronously can build even stronger social ties and create a greater sense of well-being. Crew rowing, line dancing, choir singing or simply tapping fingers in sync increases generosity, trust, and tolerance toward others" (Marta Zaraska, "Moving in Sync Creates Surprising Social Bonds," *Scientific American*, October 1, 2020. https://www.scientificamerican.com/article/moving-in-sync-creates-surprising-social-bonds-among-people/).

In this same article, Laura Cirelli, a psychologist and synchrony researcher at the University of Toronto, says that the reason for the extra affinity created by simultaneous, coordinated movement is only recently becoming understood. Studying the complicated interplay between neurohormonal, cognitive, and perceptual factors, researchers are finding evidence that our propensity for synchrony may have become part of our human evolution for the survival advantage of being bonded with large numbers of people at once.

In their 2015 article "The New Science of Singing Together," Jacques Launay and Eiluned Pearce published some research that affirms the ice breaker effect of singing that promotes fast cohesion between unfamiliar individuals. Singing together, they write, "not only helps forge social bonds, it also does so particularly quickly, acting as an excellent icebreaker." The article also asserts that "community singing is effective for bonding large groups, making it an ideal behavior to improve our broader social networks." It has also been scientifically proven that whether chanting, singing, drumming, or clapping, when we are doing things together, it strengthens our bond. As a result, people are much more likely to be more cooperative, more self-sacrificing, and more trusting of others when they experience the same rhythmic activity together (Jacques Launay and Eiluned Pearce, "The New Science of Singing Together," *Greater Good Magazine*, The Greater Good Science Center, The University University of California, Berkeley, December 4, 2015. https://greatergood.berkeley.edu/article/item/science_of_singing).

Going a little bit further down this rabbit hole, we find some interesting studies that point to the idea that the "happiest" people, as a whole, are the ones who trust and are trusted. According to the April 2022 United Nations World Happiness Report (which uses data from Gallup world polls of how people feel about their lives), Finland, the undisputed happiest country in the world, also has the world's highest level of interpersonal trust. Finland has consistently ranked number one in this category, including in 2024, which marked the seventh year in a row it was ranked number one.

Happiness expert Benjamin Radcliff, a professor of political science at the University of Notre Dame, says that "people's quality of life improves when they can reasonably assume the goodwill of others in their day-to-day lives." He adds that this more generalized interpersonal trust then filters out to more specific kinds of trust, such as trust in government. Radcliff also says that fostering trust also helps conserve emotional energy for nurturing relationships rather than worrying about the intentions of others (Benjamin Radcliff, "Trusting societies are overall happier, and a happiness expert explains why," *New Hampshire Bulletin*, https://newhampshirebulletin.com/2022/05/12/

trusting-societies-are-overall-happier-and-a-happiness-expert-explains-why-commentary/).

So you can see, if shared experiences of music or some other kind of synchronous rhythmic activity creates trust, and trust creates happiness, and happy people are more likely to assume the goodwill of others, wouldn't an emphasis on music and other synchronous activities be a good thing to add to the mix as a way to help your flock stem and resolve the interpersonal conflict so common in churches?

Do You Know What I Mean?

- Do you remember a time when you felt deeply connected to other people through a shared experience of music? How did that feel?

- When have you observed this connection in others, particularly in a worship setting?

- How could you use music differently to enhance the experience of worship and connection for the people you lead?

CHAPTER 11
Reclaim the Practice of Rest

"How can I rest when there's so much to do?"

■

"David, are you resting?"

This question came from a friend of mine, Pastor Juan Constantino. I was in Peru working with the leaders of some great larger organizations—ministries that have 30,000 to 60,000 people per week in attendance. Juan's question took me aback, both due to its off-the-wall directness and because it was uncanny he had asked; I had told no one of my recent personal struggles and my subsequent discoveries about the life-changing nature of rest. Seeing my puzzled expression in response to his question, Juan's face broke into a big smile and he said, "David, you know it's one of the Ten Commandments, right?"

I then learned from Juan about his own experience with rest—and how it led to his creating a sanctuary for church leaders and their spouses to go for a week to learn how to rest. This made me think about how many heavily burdened leaders of ministries, and so many others doing God's work in the world, neglect this very important commandment. I found out most of the worship spaces we were going to work with on this trip were led by pastors who had done this rest sabbatical with Juan and his wife Anita. Because they so loved this experience, they had invited Juan to come and teach the rest of their staff.

An Unsung Irony of Church Leadership

This may sound obvious, but you might be surprised at how few church leaders actually get the rest they need to be at their optimal effectiveness. What I learned from both my experience with Juan in Peru and listening to various lectures about rest is that when we are facing a fight or a task, or even just a choice, rest is always the right answer.

I know what you're thinking: "How can I rest when there's so much to do?" Well, that is where your thinking has gone wrong. The world takes you to the brink, but the divine leads you to safe pastures and cool, calm waters.

The Bible is full of references about rest, but in our hurry-scurry world these messages are easy to overlook. We always have that list of what we think needs to be done today, and rest is rarely, if ever, included. In a busy ministry, there is never enough time to rest, never enough time to get it all taken care of. When serving the needs of others feels more important than our own rest, it's easy to fall into the trap of "just one more hour," "just one more weekend," "just one more late night"—and *then* I'll honor that commandment to rest.

Returning to our sheep and shepherd analogy, church leaders are on a journey. The Lord is our shepherd, walking with us and leading us where we need to go. In Psalm 23, we find God's promise to provide for our needs. No matter where our earthly journey leads each of us, God has already been there and knows the way. That's not to say the journey won't be demanding, hectic, and busy. As each of us travels our own journey, we will get wrapped up in the minutiae of the journey itself.

So, in Psalm 23, when the psalmist talks about God making him lie down in green pastures and God leading him beside still waters, the Bible speaks to the need we all have for stillness. We are *made* to lie down because we get so wrapped up in the day-to-day demands of a busy life of ministry that we forget what's most important. God, our shepherd, wants us to have a rhythm in our lives between work and rest, striving and relaxing, doing and being. And, when the psalmist says, "He restores my soul," this can also be translated as, "I come to life again" or "He gives new life to me."

Just as any shepherd worth his salt leads his sheep to green pastures where they can lie down and rest, and beside still waters for refreshment and safe crossing (not the rushing waters where their wool might fill with water and they might drown), so does our Good Shepherd lead us to be still, to refresh and take time to have our souls restored.

One of my other favorite references to our need for rest, and what rest actually does for us, is in Psalm 46, where we are reminded about the importance of stillness: "Be still and know that I am God." When we're thinking about the role rest plays in our own faith and in our role as shepherd for others, this one tiny line packs a wallop. Just taking the time to be still and listen is a tall order in most days of ministry, especially for someone in any sort of leadership position.

When we're spending day after day running around, getting things done, and striving to do more, more, more—for God—isn't it ironic that the *one* thing God asks for us to do is *be still?* Being still is how we know God and how we are able to discern what God wants us to do next in our lives and ministries. By taking time to rest—to be still and know God—we can take stock of our lives and see more clearly where God wants us to go in ministry and in life.

It's Really That Simple

Years ago, I was struggling with life. You could call it a midlife crisis, or maybe things just weren't going quite the way I had planned and envisioned. I experienced what I like to call "a wilderness time" for a few years. I was running a million miles per hour, spinning my wheels, scrambling for a foothold. What felt like the last straw was a family member suddenly in need, causing me to make a really long road trip by myself to help out.

I didn't realize it at the time, but looking back now I realize I was broken. Not because my life was all that bad. Believe me, I had endured much worse stretches of struggle. What I was experiencing at that time was a random assortment of first world problems for sure. But still, after a few years of very hard work that seemed to be all for naught, it felt like nothing was going like it should. So, I'm on this long, solo road trip, and I remembered a recording that another family member had given me (and would likely soon be asking me about) that I had put off listening to.

"Why not now?" I thought, as I popped that Graham Cooke CD into the player in my car so I could say honestly that I had listened to it if they asked. Then I listened. And I listened again. And then again.

Each time I listened to this recording, different things began jumping out at me, telling me *why* I was in this place I did not want to be in. I was not resting.

You Can't Ever Catch Lost Sleep

For anyone committed to and passionate about their work, the finite number of hours in a day and days in a week can be both disappointing and frustrating. There just never seem to be enough of either to get everything done you feel you need to do to be "caught up." The temptation for most of us when these feelings arise is to borrow a few hours of sleep here and there. You know what I'm talking about—that magical time late, late at night or early, early in the morning when the rest of the world is asleep (or at least quiet). The house activities are stilled, and your phone isn't ringing. You *finally* have enough peace to hear yourself think. The urge to use this time for work can be powerful. Don't we always have the full intent of catching up on lost sleep later? I've often told myself, "I'll take a nap if I get tired." Maybe you've formed the habit of telling yourself, you'll only work through one more weekend or day off—just to catch up—so you can relax. Have you noticed that you never catch up, feel more relaxed, or replace that lost sleep?

An April 23, 2022, article "Sleepless and selfish: Lack of sleep makes us less generous" by Robert Sanders at the University of California, Berkeley, cites a study that resulted in a new discovery about lack of sleep that goes beyond the well-documented increased risk of cardiovascular disease, depression, diabetes, hypertension, and overall mortality. It will make you, as a ministry leader, stop in your tracks and rethink your lack of quality shuteye.

According to Sanders, researchers found that in addition to increasing physical health risks, "lack of sleep also impairs our basic social conscience, making us withdraw our desire and willingness to help other people." Moreover, building on twenty years of researching the link between sleep health and mental health, the study documents damage beyond the health of the sleep-deprived individual: The lack of consistent, quality sleep "degrades social interactions between individuals and, furthermore, degrades the very fabric of human society itself. How we operate as a social species—and we are a social species—seems profoundly dependent on how much sleep we are getting."

Sanders goes on to explain that in three separate studies by the same researchers, the areas of the brain that form the *theory of mind network* (ToMN)—the brain regions activated during social cognition and mental inference, which are engaged when people empathize with others or try to understand the wants and needs of others—were markedly impaired in sleep-deprived individuals. According to Eti Ben Simon, one of the study researchers quoted in Sanders's article, "When we think about other people, this network engages and allows us to comprehend what other person's needs are. What are they thinking about? Are they in pain? Do they need help? . . . It's as though these parts of the brain fail to respond when we are trying to interact with other people after not getting enough sleep."

When the researchers measured the quality of their subjects' sleep (how long they slept, how many times they woke up) and then assessed their desire to help others (such as holding an elevator door open for someone else, volunteering, or helping an injured stranger on the street—you know, basic ministry 101), they found that a decrease in the quality of someone's sleep from one night to the next predicted a significant decrease in the desire to help other people from one subsequent day to the next. "Those with poor sleep the night prior were the ones that reported being less willing and keen to help others the following day" (Robert Sanders, "Sleepless and selfish: Lack of sleep makes us less generous," *Berkeley News*, August 23, 2022. https://news.berkeley.edu/2022/08/23/sleepless-and-selfish-lack-of-sleep-makes-us-less-generous).

Any more questions about this most basic form of rest?

Sabbath Rest

Going back my earlier *"aha!"* moment in Peru about rest actually being one of the Ten Commandments, I want to dig into that a bit more. Some have called the fourth commandment listed in Exodus 20 ("Remember the Sabbath day and keep it holy") the most ignored of the commandments.

In his book *Grace & Peace: A Daily Guide for Deepening Faith,* United Methodist pastor Dr. Tim Burster says that in addition to being a day off to rest for people and animals, the Old Testament uses the word *Sabbath* to describe rest for dirt. (As in, don't plant the same crop season after season; give the field a Sabbath, a time to restore its productivity.)

There have been many interpretations of what *keeping the Sabbath day holy* really means. Orthodox Jewish traditions outline the thirty-nine categories of Sabbath work prohibited by biblical law as listed in the Mishnah (a written collection of Jewish oral tradition) and the Talmud (a central text of Jewish law). Jesus later addresses these restricted activities in the second chapter of the Gospel of Mark, saying, "The Sabbath was made for humankind, and not humankind for the Sabbath." And finally, in that familiar passage of creation in the first chapter of the book of Genesis, we read that God finished creating the universe on the sixth day of creation and then rested on the seventh day from all that work.

If even God, who is all-powerful, rests, why shouldn't we? God's gift of the Sabbath means there is one day each week set aside for us to rest. (The word *holy* actually means "set apart for a special purpose.") Within scripture we also find less of a law and more of a principle: Remember your holy time, guard your holy time, and set apart time for the special purpose of rest.

In the New Testament, Jesus invites *all* who are weary and carrying heavy burdens to come to him and he will give them rest. For church leaders and those who spend their lives in ministry to others, this oft-ignored invitation needs to be elevated to priority status. In purposefully using our gift of the Sabbath to be restored and renewed, we are better able to assess where we are in alignment with God's plan for our lives and our part in God's story.

Active Rest

Rest in this context—as time set aside to better-align ourselves with God—goes beyond taking an afternoon nap when we're tired (although that could be part of it) or getting enough quality sleep at night (also important), or meditating more (also good), or taking our allotted days off or enjoying earned vacation days (we all need breaks), or even taking a bit of time to sit still and just *be* when navigating a tough situation (to help gather thoughts and regroup).

British ministry consultant and author Graham Cooke—the one whose CD I listened to over and over on that really long road trip—says this kind of rest is better described as trust: the active trust that God is in control, and we are not. This kind of trust is leaning into the understanding that God *always* loves us fully—100 percent—in our moments of perceived failure, in our self-created circumstances, in our frustrations, and even in our biggest mistakes. The kicker is that God *also* loves us fully—100 percent—in our greatest moments and in our biggest accomplishments. God loves us 100 percent, 100 percent of the time, regardless of what we do or don't do, and have or haven't accomplished.

Of course, God loves us no matter what. We know that. We also most certainly know that God is in control. It's not like we haven't heard this for most of our Christian walk. Some of us have heard this all our lives. What I'm talking about here is beyond hearing it, knowing it, believing it, or even experiencing it. This new dimension of understanding is *acting upon it*. Living our lives *embracing* this truth. This, as it turns out, makes the critical difference.

Digging into this idea of active rest a bit more, I was fascinated to learn that rest is often the deciding factor in most battles. The well-rested army wins the day. The downtrodden, tired, weakened, confused troops tend to make bad choices and spiral. The well-rested troops are more confident, stronger, and have made better choices to prepare.

When we're slogging through something, with with poor self-care (lack of sleep, wallowing in self-pity, unhealthy coping with trauma, past guilt, or whatever other "life stuff" has beaten us down), it can be hard to remember that God is a comfort we can go to for rest when the going gets tough. Learning to retreat from emotional struggle and rest for a while in the arms of God will give us what we need to go on. By settling into this holy space, we can allow ourselves to remember that God has things under control. All the pain and second-guessing clouding our mind disappears. When we're resting in God's control, we become more focused, our brain works better, we are more creative, and we emerge ready to go back into whatever we're facing.

We don't have to take on whatever difficulty or challenge we're going through alone. We don't have to hold all that anxiety and unrest—that's a terrible place to be. There is always a place to rest, to set down our burdens, and to regain what we need to move forward in whatever work God has given us to do.

Rest in Trust

The concept of resting in trust was strange to me at first. If you tend to be nervous, feel anxious, and get all keyed up when things feel out of control, you are neglecting the active rest that is perhaps better described as trust. We are not always (if ever) fully privy to God's plans. At best, it's more of a need-to-know basis type thing, and it doesn't seem like God feels we need to know. God will sometimes offer a glimpse or a vision, but at the end of the day, God asks for our trust.

This is not as easy as it sounds. Most leaders are also control freaks (that's often how they became leaders in the first place!) who at some point got attached to a vision that God gave them at that time. Pretty soon they started thinking of that vision, from God, as their own vision, and then the worry set in about not completing the vision.

When we as leaders start making the vision personal, what we are missing is the freedom we'd feel if we were *resting* in trust. If God tells us we should build a church or start a business, and we get to work doing as asked, we all at some point take responsibility and control of that vision. You start working longer and longer hours and focus more and more on the tasks at hand, even to the point of neglecting friends and family for this mission, this goal you have set.

Notice that I said "this goal *you* have set." God asked only for you to build it. It was *you* who took it further, assuming the ask was to build the largest, most powerful influential place for doing God's work. This is still a good and noble thing, and of course your motives are still pure, but can you see how things start going off track? God just requested that you build it. You're the one who started stressing about the details, stability, and longevity of it. What if God just wanted you to build it? What if God's plan for you is to then move on to something else?

Who's the Hero in Your Story?

Many great things are built on the backs of the nameless—those who are nameless on Earth but saints and heroes in heaven, those who will hear Jesus say, as is written in Matthew 25, "Well done, good and faithful servant."

Imagine you are the person who is supposed to build a church, and you understand that the purpose of your building this church is for it to help people for however long it can. And, in addition, there is one special purpose of this church, and unbeknownst to you, that sole purpose is to help a single individual, just one person. One sermon you deliver in this church will flip the switch in this individual's young mind and help lead this person to do great things. Perhaps a kind word the Holy Spirit used you to deliver will keep that person from dying by suicide, something that may have been planned for that very day, and that person instead went on to fulfill God's great plan for their life.

The interesting thing about how God works in our lives is that we never know what ultimate good our work will do in the life of someone else. We may never know what stories we are part of until Jesus tells us face-to-face. The secret is learning to rest in our trust that God is in control, and we are part of stories we are not going to be aware of.

I heard a sermon one day that asked: What if your whole life is leading to one moment? Think about that. What if your role in God's great story is to be like Red Leader, the heroic Star Wars pilot who built the team, came up with the plan, and flew his X-Wing fighter in an attempt to destroy the Death Star (and died in the process), providing Luke the opportunity to be tested in his faith? What if your role in someone else's story is to show that something spiritually bigger is at play than just human prowess and technology? Would all your hard work to become a leader and pilot, planning and fighting the battles and building the team that got everyone to this point, be worth it if you couldn't be the one who made the winning shot?

The truth is we don't know what God's exact plans are for our lives. We only know as far as we can see in this moment. Like following the beam of a flashlight when you're walking outdoors at night, you can only see what's in the beam, and not beyond. But, as you move, so does the beam, lighting your next steps and showing you any twists and turns in the trail you didn't know about before. When we walk in God's light, staying active in our trust, we know where we are in each moment and what the next few steps will be. Where our active rest— and trust— comes into play is when we have to be okay knowing that, in the end, God's will is going to be done, even if we don't quite know what God's will is.

As Christians, we really don't have to worry about the Lord's will being done. That's not what keeps us up at night, not what we have anxiety about. Because we don't know our part in the plan, we are called to trust and move forward as God calls us to. But it's hard to hear God's voice when we're so busy scurrying around trying to accomplish what we *think* is important. I know that *true rest* will come to me when I trust that God loves me and has set me on a path to do the work God wants to do through me. That takes a lot of stress off, doesn't it? This is the type of rest most of us are missing. Easy to talk about, even easy to understand, but a continuous day-to-day challenge to execute. We give our trust, and then we take it back again. It's our nature. God loves us through it and asks us, gently, to try again.

I hear what you're thinking: What if I know God has given me a job to do—and there are so many parts to it that it all feels urgent. What if I fail? The word *I* is key to the answer to this question, which, for most of us, is a persistent one. When we do our part as we understand it, to the best of our ability, that is all God asks of us. If the task is too big for you to do alone, you may just be one leg of the relay. You may not be the one to take a person all the way to the promised land, or the one who hears that the Holy Spirit changed this person's life and spoke the words of salvation. You might just be the one who takes someone to the gate, sows the seed, reveals the path. That's okay. When we find ourselves worrying about getting it done, we need to stop and remember: God's will *will* be done. It just may not look or be the way we imagined it.

I have had many conversations over the years that were just a step in a process, and I'm proud to be a part of that step. I have had people come back to me, years later, telling me that something we talked about set them on a different path, and these are just the people I happened to see again. I know *I* didn't change those people's lives, and I'm fine with that. I'm not interested in arguing people into a conversion just to get them to say the words that give me reason to say "Yep! Saved another one!" Only the Holy Spirit can make a conversion. Sometimes we get to be there and play our part when called to do so.

What about when we have legitimate worries, such as financial, career, and relationship issues? It's very hard to rest when demands are closing in, and things must be done to take care of these concerns. What my studies and meditations have taught me about active rest is this: When we deliberately budget time to actively rest in the Lord, and get to know and recognize the nudges of Holy Spirit, the choices we make are better. When life's challenges bombard us, we are ready to face them with the full knowledge and comfort that God is with us as we play our part—run the race that is ours to run—in God's unfolding story.

Remember the Pendulum

In Chapter 5: Unpack How People Respond and Chapter 9: Guide the Experience, we talked a bit about the concept of the pendulum when it comes to aligning with God's direction for our lives. Remember, the pendulum has a weight at the bottom, some sort of balancing mechanism, a center point, and long point at the top. At rest, a pendulum stays straight up and down, as a straight and true line to the target.

When you think of your life as a pendulum, and the straight and true line as your connection with God and God's plan for your life, the place of rest is at that center. When opposing forces on either side push against the bottom of the pendulum, a challenge arises. When one side pushes, the top goes off-center in the opposite direction. If the other side pushes, the top goes off-center in the other direction. If they push equally and meet in the middle, the alignment returns. Finding that place of balance keeps us at that resting center, aligned with God.

That's rest. Staying in the middle. When you find yourself trying to get it all done, pushing your life off-kilter, letting other things take control of your life, worrying too much about the wants and needs of others, trying to accomplish more, do more, and follow others' opinions, you'll push the bottom of the pendulum back and forth, one way or the other. Go back to the quiet center, into rest. Let God tell you where to put your mind and your energy.

Listen for the voice of the Good Shepherd. The voice of love, the voice of encouragement, the voice that calls you to the place of rest. (If the voice you're hearing, thinking about, and following makes you feel worse about yourself, it's not the right voice.) If you need to work on something, it's said in a loving way, such as: "Once you do this, you can have that—and won't that be great?" This is the voice that is calling you to growth, trust, access, and opportunity you wouldn't otherwise have had. If you're having trouble hearing this voice of encouragement, it's typically because *you* moved away, not God.

To move back to resting in God, quiet your mind. Listen. The voice is still there, still talking, still loving you wherever you are. The challenge is identifying what's in the way of your hearing it, and removing that obstacle, whatever it is. Easy to say—and so hard to do.

Do You Know What I Mean?

- When was the last time you felt truly rested? When in the rhythm of your weeks do you allow yourself this level of rest? What could you do to improve your weekly rest?

- How do you encourage the people you lead to rest? Do you insist on it or try to enforce mandatory days off?

- When have you experienced rest more as trust? When have you run into the comforting arms of God to get the rest you need and the assurance to carry on? What would it take to remember that as an option when you feel really overwhelmed?

CHAPTER 12
Remember Your Why

In the end, you are the one responsible for carrying the voice of love to your flock.

■

Why did you choose a career in ministry? This seems like an obvious question, but do you really know? Can you say without thinking *why* you do what you do? What do *you* get out of doing ministry? Even though on the surface this last question may look a bit selfish, I see this question—and its honest answer—as necessary to knowing what fills you up. You can only go for so long on your own power, and it is crucial for your long-term well-being to know what and where your filling station is. God wants to fill your tank with all sorts of great things, and this shows up differently for everyone. A full tank for you may or may not mean wealth or an easy life, but it definitely does mean joy and peace beyond our understanding. It also means a purpose and structure that will fulfill you if you let them.

This question, if you're honest with yourself, can also bring out some of the wrong reasons for being in ministry, too. This makes for a good place to search your heart and soul, evaluate your motives, and check your pendulum to see if everything lines up before you try to lead others.

What's Your Goal?

People who spend their lives and careers in some type of ministry want to feel they are making a difference. But how? There has to be a goal. What's yours? What is your team's goal? We are spending a lot of time and energy getting people in the door and engaged in God's work. We are helping them to find a place where God will do something special through them. What exactly are we trying to accomplish? What special things are *we* supposed to be doing? What's *God's* agenda for these people we're shepherding? You're probably not in ministry just because you like hanging out at church. There's something you hope to see happen. What is it?

When I first begin working with ministry teams, it's often very hard for people to articulate what they want to accomplish in their leadership. Often, this question is tossed to a team of people with differing ideas of exactly what they're trying to accomplish—with no real authority to make things happen.

I think it is absolutely essential to focus on these questions from the biblical perspective. If I'm going to know where we're going as a church or organization, I'd better understand the heart of God. Why did God create church in the first place? What is it here for? What role could *this* ministry play in that mission? These answers can be different from ministry to ministry, so we've got to be sure to be consistent with what God gave the church to do.

Many pieces of scripture talk about the purpose of the church. There's a lot on this topic in Ephesians and some more in the Gospels, where Jesus seems to be sending those early disciples on very particular missions. Was all this instruction and advice from Jesus just for the start-up? Are we, the disciples of today, supposed to be doing something else?

If the cornerstone is still Jesus, and he was tasked with presenting God in human form to the world, and those first twelve disciples were tasked with the same thing, wouldn't all that still apply to the rest of us, even now? If you go back to the New Testament and read through the early chapters of Acts, you'll find people who fully believed that they were there for one purpose and one purpose only: to carry Jesus Christ into the world so people would know him, be drawn to him, have their lives transformed, and carry forth this work to others.

Isn't that still true? Isn't that what *we* are here for? It seems to me that if that same purpose is really what the church is here for—its one true-north priority—having four or five or six additional purposes seems kind of extra, doesn't it? Let's get back to *your* ministry. (That *is* why you're still reading this book, right?) How does what you're doing in ministry today line up with that original, true-north priority? In the complexities of today's world, it's easy to get caught up in all the extras. We think we need to innovate more and more to get people's attention.

With all the different styles of Christian ministry, there's a lot of competition out there. How can your ministry stand out from the rest and entice people to join your flock? In this frenzied environment, it's easy for churches to lose sight of that one, true-north priority. When we find ourselves off-center, how can we regain that essential balance? How can we keep "true north" front and center as our priority in the face of all the temptation to subscribe to the societal need for all the extras?

Well, you've got a group of people who have been brought to you by the grace of God. People in whom God uniquely dwells. These people have been purposefully placed where they are, in their own little places in the world—their schools, their jobs, their neighborhoods—because there's something extraordinary God wants to do *through them* to carry love and grace into the world. God has also put you where *you* are on purpose. You are in the exact place you need to be to reach these people with the truth of the Gospels. This can be transformative for them and for all the people they meet.

That's your why, and it's unique to you. You're the person God chose for the situation you're in. All you have to do is move forward with this divine blessing and do what you were put here to do. Can you think of anything more important?

It's All About Love

So, how do these ideas all come together? What should you take away from this book that will most benefit you, your ministry, and the people you lead? We've talked about some fun things, some hard things, and some abstract things (my favorite), and now I want to land this plane with a life-changing (or at least thought-provoking) concept that really benefits you and your ministry.

God knows how we are wired and how the world will try to beat us into submission and eventual death. God put plenty of evidence in the scientific world for us to use, both positive and negative, to help make sense of our world. And yet, none of this evidence makes life any easier, because across an array of situations and tasks, we almost always hear negativity louder than we do positivity. It's what the National Institutes of Health calls *negativity bias*, or "the propensity to attend to, learn from, and use negative information far more than positive information" (Amrisha Vaish, Tobias Grossmann, and Amanda Woodward, "Not all emotions are created equal: The negativity bias in social-emotional development," National Library of Medicine, https://www.ncbi.nlm.nih.gov/pmc/articles/PMC3652533/).

In addition to this tendency to lean into negative thoughts, (which some place as high as 70 percent of all our waking conscious thought), our typical default is to try to be as safe as possible. We want to stay under the social radar, not do anything that will embarrass us or draw attention to our shortcomings. We want to stay safe in our pack or tribe. We tend to try to hide our true selves, or only show a small part of ourselves to others and hide the rest. (If we let too much of ourselves show, we might get kicked out of the club.) Sometimes we surround ourselves with people we feel a little above or better than, or with people who won't push us, call us out, or ostracize us. Heaven knows we do enough of that to ourselves. (I know for sure I am harder on myself than on anyone else in the world, sometimes fearmongering myself into procrastination and even shutdown!)

Managing Personal Mythology

If you don't know my personal story, I had a pretty hard time growing up, dealing with a few disabilities, being bullied by teachers and peers, and even getting mentally and physically beat up by the medical community. Being a fighter by nature, I pushed through. I learned to use the anger, hurt, and "scripts" from the past to beat myself into the form I thought would serve me best. While the details changed through the years, the process of using the stories I told myself to pivot and reinvent remained the same.

I found a tribe, defined a purpose, discovered some things I excelled at, and pressed on to show everyone I was not who they said I was—an oversized, dumb, loser who would never amount to anything. I finally understood that running from my past hurts, shoving the pain down, and chasing what I thought was success to feel validated was not sustainable. These behaviors and patterns were not of love. They were fear-based or pride-based (and sometimes a combination of the two), fueled by the feeling of "I'll show *them*!"

Now, don't get me wrong. These strategies did work for a time. I was allowed to do some amazing things and be a part of some fantastic adventures, and through it all, God still used me—but I was broken. I was hurt. I was putting up a lot of fake confidence while underneath I was constantly tearing myself apart and beating myself up. When things were good, I could only acknowledge the win for a moment, just enough to push off for more. No win was ever enough. *I* was never enough. Can you relate? Have you ever felt like an imposter when things were going well?

Years ago, I had really turned my world upside down. I was in a very bad place, and I felt like everything was crashing down around me. While I had enjoyed some success, was getting pretty well-known in my field of work, and it looked like everything was going great, I also had a few huge failures in a row. The fear of more failure had me completely paralyzed. Again. I had very little faith in myself. Not in my work. Not in my life. I still had faith in God, but I would find a way to beat myself up for that, too. Whenever I'd think about my faith in God, a crushing voice within me would tell me I wasn't doing enough and that I should be doing more to show people my faith.

We all have our personal mythology—the stories we tell ourselves about ourselves. About our life. About the events that have shaped and continue to shape us. About our successes and failures, our strengths, and our shortcomings. And ultimately, about what these things really mean and the importance they hold in the overarching narrative of our life.

What's *your* personal mythology? How will you manage it?

An Unexpected Lifeline

When I found myself on yet another emergency road trip, this time to save a dog, I listened to another of British ministry consultant Graham Cooke's CDs, this time a training program renowned for its practical applications for living a life of faith. This seminar changed my perspective forever. In addition to emphasizing the importance of rest (as we explored in Chapter 11), Cooke says that *having faith* is not the issue. *Love* is the issue. Once you truly know how much you are loved, faith is never a problem. He also says that when you really *know* that Jesus loves you—that he has no illusions about you, he knows everything you are thinking (good, bad, and otherwise), and he still fully and deeply loves you—it's a game changer. Understanding that no matter what happens or doesn't happen, Jesus will *still* love you 100 percent removes a huge amount of pressure when you're stuck, when you've succeeded, and especially when you've failed.

For me, being able to grasp—and hold onto—this love from God that never changes, never decreases, and never ends, makes faith so much easier. When trouble comes (and it *will* come), you *know* you can depend on the voice full of love, laughter, peace, and joy to guide and support you through it. Faith takes fear out of life. It invites you to run into the arms of this all-encompassing love when that old negativity bias starts to take over.

Suddenly, it all started making sense to me. God, Christ, and the Holy Spirit all speak the same language. They all bear the same fruit the apostle Paul refers to in the fifth chapter of Galatians as "the Fruit of the Spirit," which includes love, joy, peace, patience, kindness, generosity, faithfulness, gentleness, and self-control.

If you imagine God talking to Jesus, do you think God would use the kind of crushing words you hear when you talk to yourself? Do you speak those crushing words to someone you love? Would you *ever* speak to anyone in the same manner that you speak to yourself? Have you ever said to yourself things like:

>"I can't believe you ate that."
>"You are terrible to think that."
>"You're so weak you can't even [fill in the blank]."
>"You'll never be the person you should be."
>"Why even bother?"
>"Well, Stupid, you did it again."
>"You're so frustrating!"
>"Why can't you ever get it right?"
>"You know better."
>"I can't believe you did [or didn't] do that!"

Do you hear these kinds of words sometimes in your head when you're talking to yourself? Can you even imagine saying these kinds of things to someone you care about? If you were only allowed to speak to yourself using the Fruit of the Spirit as your guide, how would you rephrase your self-talk? Imagine how different it would feel if:

"I can't believe you ate that" becomes
"That's okay, you'll make a better choice next time."

"You are terrible to think that" becomes
"We all have thoughts we're not proud of. How can you reframe that in a more positive way?"

"You're so weak you can't even [fill in the blank]" becomes
"You'll get there if you keep working at it."

"You'll never be the person you should be" becomes
"Improvement happens day by day; just keep doing your best."

"Why even bother" becomes
"Every little bit of progress makes a difference in the long run."

"Well, Stupid, you did it again" becomes
"Everyone makes mistakes; how can you use this one to learn and grow?"

"You're so frustrating" becomes
"It's hard to be patient, but I'm worth it."

"Why can't you ever get it right" becomes
"What can you learn from this, so it won't happen again?"

"You know better" becomes
"It's okay. Slip-ups happen. Now get back on track."

"I can't believe you did [or didn't] do that" becomes
"It's okay. You'll do it next time, and if there isn't a next time, you'll figure out how to make the best of it.

Love, Laughter, Encouragement, Hope—and Peace

This idea of learning to rephrase or reframe the things I say to myself was the kicker for me! With plenty of time to think after hearing Cooke's presentation, I realized some important truths as if for the first time. The shepherd's voice is kind. It feels safe—and that's why the sheep listen for it, attune their ears, and follow! If it were a tense, angry voice filled with rage and venom, do you think any animal would respond in a positive way?

The horse, dog, and sheep whisperers' ways work, because they mimic what God was saying to the shepherds who lived with and loved those animals in biblical times. Christ's voice is in line with the Fruit of the Spirit. This is how Christ talks. It's the encouraging voice we listen for, the one that reminds us we are loved and meant to have peace within us, not driven to distraction by the voice that crushes and beats us up. It's a happy, joyful voice that is glad to see us, glad that we have come, excited to show us new things. It's the voice that gives us opportunities to grow, laugh, and love others in this manner too. It is the voice that is safe above all else. This is the voice that makes you want to follow joyfully into good and healthy things. This is the voice of God. All other voices (of fear, anger, frustration, resentment, and other negatives) we need to push away so we can focus instead on what's good, encouraging, and reassuring.

That is the baseline of good self-talk. At the very least, you should to talk to yourself with the level of kindness you would extend to a stranger you don't know. At best, you should talk to yourself as you would talk to a person you care *deeply* about. Would you say those negative things to a stranger or someone you care about? No, of course you wouldn't. (If you would, well, that's a different conversation!) That would just be mean, right? So why would you ever say those kinds of things to yourself? It's also worth noting that if you're saying destructive, hurtful, negative things to yourself, it is more than likely you are inflicting these judgments on your closest circles, including your family.

Just Listen to Yourself

How do we break these habits of negative self-talk? Start by taking a step back to observe yourself. Be still. Listen. Do the thoughts flowing through your head have voices that are less than friendly and supportive? Talk to others, ask questions, and see what triggers you. Then do the reframing work to ease that trigger.

When you need some help with this, pray for God's love, remember love, and remember you are loved unconditionally by your Creator. Then start intentionally adjusting the way you talk to yourself. Start adjusting the way that you talk to other people, too. Turn everything upside down. Make it so that you are nicest to yourself—and your family as an extension—then move outward to being nice to strangers. Make this your true self everywhere, inside and out.

Yes, you are responsible for your actions and there needs to be discipline in your life. I'm not giving you a pass to mess up, to not do what you're supposed to, or to be irresponsible! You will still need to work hard, and sometimes do hard things. Sometimes bad things will happen, just like sometimes good things will happen. All I am saying is, just make sure that even when you're noticing things that you could do better, or acknowledging things you have done wrong, or when you're thinking about mistakes you have made, be sure that your words to yourself *no matter what happens* are wrapped in love, kindness, peace, and maybe even a little gratitude and joy.

In the end, you are the one responsible for carrying the voice of love to your flock. If you're willing to do the work of getting still enough to observe it, hear it, recognize it, and follow it—no matter what else is going on in the world—you will become the shepherd your flock can count on.

Do You Know What I Mean?

- What got you into ministry in the first place? How has your path remained connected to that original response to God's call?

- What stories do you tell yourself about your ministry journey that have become part of your personal mythology? If you were to rewrite one of these stories, how would you change it?

- If you're able to monitor your inner critic (many people have to work on this skill), what kinds of things do you habitually say to yourself when you're not deliberately focusing on "positive self-talk?" Are these words kind and constructive? Can you imagine God speaking to Jesus that way?

- How do you find inner stillness? (Sometimes the only way we can get inwardly still is to be physically active—walking, running, cycling, etc.) What daily habit could you cultivate to just. be. still. for some portion every single day in order to connect more intentionally with God?

AFTERWORD
Now that You Know Sheep

We've come to the end of our sheep trail through a deep exploration of the job of shepherd. A shepherd's whole life is about taking care of the sheep. It's all-consuming. The sheep become like extended family. They are also a shepherd's livelihood—and the shepherd's legacy. Sheep can be difficult. They get themselves into trouble. They count on their shepherd to show them the way.

Let's review and reflect on the overarching ideas of this book—and how you might apply them in your own life of ministry.

Sheep Follow the Shepherd's Voice.

Just as you listen for and discern the voice of God, the people you lead listen for your voice. They depend on you to be true to God's calling on your life and to offer that influence as it pertains to their own path. They depend on your pendulum to be in the balanced center, and for you to show them the way forward, especially when situations challenge your church and its people as individuals. It is the business of every shepherd to know the sheep, individually and collectively. The shepherd knows best how to care for them, what they need, how they behave, what motivates them, what frightens them, and how to manage them effectively when the unanticipated, unpredictable, and unsettling things inevitably happen to them in the course of their lives.

How well do you know your sheep, collectively and individually?

What do you do on a consistent basis (other than weekly sermons) to let them hear your voice and experience firsthand what a balanced pendulum looks like?

How much time are you spending in stillness each day, just listening for the voice of God so you can lead others by example, sharing faithfully both your questions and the guidance you receive?

Following God Takes the Pressure Off.

Once you accept that God is in control and your job is to follow your own Good Shepherd's call, you'll find ideas and access to opportunities you may never have imagined. God wants for you a life and a ministry rooted in goodness and joy, even in times that don't look or feel so good. When you learn to ask for guidance and wait for God to show you your next steps, you open yourself to new ways of being in the world. Likewise, when you realize you're not following God, but reacting to something out of fear or to avoid pain, you have the opportunity to return once again to that place of love and acceptance —of yourself and of others—and the world opens up and becomes a different place.

How do you recognize when your ego has become too invested in the vision you have for your overall ministry?

When have you had this realization and made a course correction?

Looking back on these times (that's often how we see them most clearly), what tangible difference did it make in the path you chose for those who depend on your leadership?

Sometimes the Best Form of Evangelism Is to Just Back Off.

There's a herd mentality that can run amok when it comes both to actual sheep, and to groups of people who are passionate about what they believe. Every group of people—congregation, study group, team, and staff—includes people who are harder to love. (They are almost always the ones who need it most!) One of the biggest downfalls in the church is behavior directly opposed to what Christians say they believe. In both individuals and groups, there is a my-way-or-the-highway mentality that tries to brainwash people or argue them into submission. Bound by rules that rely on flawed human insight, it's hard to see into the hearts of people who think differently. Often, both ministry and lay leaders want to make everyone see things their way (which they are pretty sure is also *God's* way), and even the most well-intentioned among them can cause harm. Modeling the behavior they seek in others could be the solution they're looking for.

Have you ever witnessed this behavior in people you are leading? How about in yourself?

When you see this kind of situation shaping up in a group you are leading, how could you inspire different behavior?

When you examine the teachings of Jesus, you see this behavior modeled time and again, but many people also feel like Jesus wants them to evangelize. How can you demonstrate the balance?

As Leaders, We Tend to Focus More on the Whole Coastline.

Looking at things from the 30,000-foot view (like a shepherd scanning the distant terrain) can be extremely helpful for making sure your organization is staying on course. However, when you try to lead by viewing only that big picture, you can miss the ins and outs of what's really going on at ground level (and you may very likely step in a hole and twist your ankle). In guiding others in ministry, the 30,000-foot view tells you nothing about what's really going on in the lives of the individuals you are leading. Without a perspective that balances these two extremes, it's easy to misstep (hole) and make decisions that can crush people, steamrolling them without realizing it. It's easy to think something is a simple black-and-white issue, when really it's shrouded in gray areas that could change everything.

When have you experienced a 30,000-foot coastline view that caused you to miss some important ins and outs of a ministry situation?

How do you consider the details without getting lost in the weeds?

When have you experienced a good balance of these extremes and experienced a positive and productive outcome that required knowledge of both perspectives?

Faith, in General, Is a Choice.

The world is full of choice. The paradox of choice is the paralysis that can come with too many choices and too much analysis. How much is enough? The solution, it seems, is building boundaries. By creating a big box around choices you face, you set boundaries that help you feel safer. Sometimes, you make a smaller box to feel even safer, and then an even smaller one. While creating boundaries and parameters offers a sense of safety, it can also be counterintuitive to your ministry goals. This is where you have to stop and think about what you're doing and why. Sometimes you need to push those boundaries back out closer to the true edges.

When have you, as a ministry leader, been overwhelmed by too many choices?

How do you typically respond when you encounter the paradox of choice?

What indicators tell you that the boxes around your ministries have grown too small and those boundaries need to be pushed back out to encompass more, not fewer, choices?

Everyone Has Their Own Drivers for How They Will Respond.

Each person's individual emotional underpinning and unique life experiences inform their reactions. In a large group of people together (a whole herd of them), each individual is thinking and interpreting everything that happens differently. The more people you have, the deeper the fractal subculture of individual experiences you will be dealing with. If you're not aware of this dynamic, the more you can get caught up and mired in the mess it creates.

How have you seen this fractal subculture play out in your own life and ministry?

How do you typically respond when you see this dynamic arising during a difficult situation in ministry—when you can see the invisible drivers of conflict?

How could you better recognize and address the gifts of these unique perspectives without allowing them to foment conflict within your ministries?

The People Most Grateful to God for the Relationship Are Often the Ones Who Have Been Forgiven the Most.

People with nothing to lose are sometimes considered "scary," but they can also be the ones who change the world. If you could do anything, with nothing to lose, what would you do?

When in your ministry have you encountered "scary people"—people with nothing to lose? How did God use that experience for good? How did that experience change you?

Do you personally identify more with someone who has nothing to lose—or with the lazy lion ready to get out of that cage and do something meaningful? If you could do anything, what would you do?

What have you done in your ministry to get yourself and your flock prepared in "God's gym" to train for the work God has for you and your organization to do?

"It's My Fault if I Don't Say It; It's Your Fault if You Don't Listen."

Continuing to love on people even when they reject what you have to say can break down barriers and actually allow that message to percolate within them. You really never know the long-term effect of your words and actions—so one of the essential skills of ministry is to continue to speak up without attachment to the result. Clamming up when you see someone do something you don't like—or worse, walking away from the person, writing them off as having nothing to offer—is rarely helpful for either of you in the long run. You'll do your best work in relationship and community, and you'll go a long way in ministry by taking to heart Jesus's advice not to judge others. While you're at it, also take to heart Jesus's reminder that we all have things to work on (and only if you're without sin can you cast a stone at someone else). Cultivating the practice of speaking up and then letting go allows the Holy Spirit to take it from there.

When have you chosen not to speak up and instead walked away from someone who opposed you? What was the result?

Have you ever experienced a miracle turnaround—a dramatic change of heart—that happened because of something you said that you may not even remember saying?

How could you be more alert to these opportunities and teach others to do the same?

Before You Lead Action, Get to Know Your Sheep.

If the idea of demographic research on your congregation and surrounding geographic area makes your eyes glaze over and has you reaching for your phone to find someone to do this drudgery for you, you might want to think again. Not only do shepherds need to know the quirks of their individual sheep, they also need a good overall picture of what they like to consume, where they like to rest, what sights and sounds they are attracted to, what scares them, and what makes them feel safe. You can have the best intentions in the world, but before you start designing logos and laying cornerstones, you have to understand the needs and desires of the people you want to reach.

How well do you know the likes, dislikes, hopes, and fears of your existing congregation? What about for those you wish to attract?

What questions reveal the things you need to know in order to make good decisions about the direction of your programs and ministries?

What can you do to shore up your personal knowledge of the demographic information and preferences of the people you serve now and wish to serve in the future?

A Strong Decision-Making Hierarchy Makes the Vision Clear for Everyone.

Today's leaders have more decisions to make—and they have to make them faster, with less time to explain—than ever before. This reality can create challenges for getting your whole team on the same page when it comes to decision-making and carrying out decisions made. Once you've clarified and honed your vision to a single priority, it's time to communicate that vision and priority to your organization and let them know that every decision made is to be measured against this single priority.

How do you typically make and communicate important directional management decisions? How about the day-to-day operational decisions?

What would it be like to have a single measurement device in place that you and everyone on your management team could use to make their ministry decisions?

Do you think offering a single measurement for every decision, large or small, could eliminate guesswork (including second-guesswork), indecision, and frustration in your organization?

A Shepherd's Choices Guide the Flock's Experience.

For actual sheep, the choices shepherds make (using their own decision trees) include plentiful green grass, clean and calm waters, shelter from storms, and safety from predators. For church leaders, the decisions that guide their flock's experience of worship are really not all that different, but operate more on a spiritual level. The worship experience you're offering those in your care will help protect and sustain them in their day-to-day lives. As they face challenges, live through hard times, and support one another, the choices you make about their worship experience actively impacts their spiritual lives.

How well is your worship space functioning now in terms of lighting, sound, video?

Are you actively guiding the worship experience using these tools of technology, or just using them in the same old way?

Have you ever been impacted in a worship service beyond the sermon and music in ways you could feel but can't articulate? How long have you carried that experience with you?

Music, a Powerful Connector.
It is well-documented that music can do things that cannot be replicated with drugs or with just about any other influence—from bridging cultural and generational gaps to evoking emotion at the deepest levels. From qualitative research on music-based interventions for people with dementia to the restorative effect of tapping into deepest music memories, it is now known that music is so much more than just something fun to listen to or something to fill the spaces in a worship service.

How are you using music in your worship and ministries now?

Could taking advantage of brain science research make your music programming more impactful?

In what new ways could you use music to help cement your ministry messages?

Getting the Rest You Need is About Much More than Effectiveness.

Just as any good shepherd leads sheep to green pastures where they can lie down and rest beside still waters for refreshment and into places of comfort and safety, so does the Good Shepherd lead us to be still, to refresh, and to take time to have our souls restored. Ministry is busy, busy, busy work—with thousands of demands pummeling its leadership day after day. If you take time to rest, how will you ever catch up? Active rest is trusting that God will sanctify and protect your times of rest—and will make sure that everything that *really* needs to get done Will Be Done.

Are you resting?

How can you change your habits and day-to-day patterns to incorporate more rest and stillness?

What will you do today to increase both the quantity and quality of your rest—and encourage all who are in ministry with you to do the same?

Why Did *You* Choose a Career in Ministry?

On the surface, the question of why you are doing ministry may sound silly, but both this question and its honest answer are necessary to knowing what fills you up. You can only go for so long on your own power, and it is crucial to your long-term well-being to know what and where your filling station is. It's also a good place to search your heart, evaluate your motives, and check your pendulum to see if everything lines up before you try to lead others.

Everyone is called to ministry of some kind. What first drew you to the particular area you're in?

What is the most meaningful experience you've had so far in ministry?

If you could change one thing about your ministry to align it more with your why, what would it be?

About the Author

A creative communicator who has served as a senior leader for several multi-million-dollar companies over the past few decades, David McCauley still spends most of his time traveling to consult and design audiovisual systems for businesses, ministries, and performance venues of all sizes and types. David has become well-known for his thought leadership, talent, and tenacity for finding optimum communication solutions, and his knowledge and influence can be seen in many venues across the nation and around the world. Beyond his accomplishments in room acoustics, audio imaging, projection, LED video, lighting, scenic design, and staging, David is revered for his problem-solving processes that empower innovative communication solutions.

Blessed with both an innate curiosity and a voracious appetite for knowledge, David has studied continuously from a young age, both formally and informally, and he has collaborated with mentors and peers along the way to acquire the knowledge base he is still expanding upon today. Shaped by his formal training in psychology and theology, David's focus on getting to the core of real-world challenges and opportunities has helped him evolve right along with the lightning-paced industry he serves. Also shaped in part by his early struggles to overcome significant learning differences, David has developed the ability to see problem-solving in new ways that create deeper understanding—and the desire to share what he has learned with others.

Over the years David has been a speaker and presenter at numerous national and international industry events, including those held by the National Association of Broadcasters, Live Design International, Infocomm, Worship Facilities Expo, and the American Institute of Architects.

Acknowledgments

To Mom and Dad, who always believed in me and tried to give me the best opportunities they could. To Mark Fair, who started me on my AV path when I was eight or nine years old and who gave me a chance to begin the learning that helped set my path. To Howard Edmondson, who befriended me—a crazy long-haired guy at a concert—showed me love, gave me the opportunity to learn and grow in spirit and humility through mentorship, and helped me get a scholarship to study theology.

I would also love to thank so many more people and mentors who have taught me and given me the strength and knowledge to be who I am today—you know who you are! You are a *huge* part of my story.

Special thanks, too, to Melinda Folse for helping me bring this long-dreamed-of book into being—and to her team at Five Crow Press for putting it into its final form.

www.ingramcontent.com/pod-product-compliance
Lightning Source LLC
Chambersburg PA
CBHW040303170426
43194CB00021B/2882